His Ingredient Label

His Ingredient Label:

A Woman's Guide to Recognizing a Junk Food Man

J. M. TARDY, MBA/PHR

iUniverse, Inc.
New York   Bloomington

His Ingredient Label
A Woman's Guide to Recognizing a Junk Food Man

iUniverse books may be ordered through booksellers or by contacting:

iUniverse
1663 Liberty Drive
Bloomington, IN 47403
www.iuniverse.com
1-800-Authors (1-800-288-4677)

ISBN: 978-1-4502-1552-7 (sc)
ISBN: 978-1-4502-1627-2 (dj)
ISBN: 978-1-4502-1553-4 (ebk)

Library of Congress Control Number: 2010902779

Printed in the United States of America

iUniverse rev. date: 04/01/2010

*This book is dedicated to my father, Richard L. Tardy, Jr.,
and to my love, Isaac W. Smith II.
Thank you for teaching me how it feels to be loved by good men.*

Contents

Acknowledgments

I would like to thank God for three things: allowing my circumstances (both good and bad) to come to pass, providing me the resilience to pull through each one, and allowing me the ability to translate my circumstances into real-life examples that may help the next person. This is my contribution.

I want to thank those who critiqued my first draft: Kadetra, Kisah, Angela, and Latoya. You deserve the award for reading this book in its original state, the brainstorming phase. My first editor, Debra, really helped smooth my fragmented thoughts in a manner that was communicable to others. I really appreciate you.

A special thanks to my mother, Elverleen, and sister, Andrea, for their endless support of every idea that evolved during the writing of this book. There were many times I would have suffered writer's block if I hadn't had you both to bounce ideas off of.

I want to thank my girlfriends, Bianca, Rae, Yolanda, and Rica, who sat back and waited patiently for the book to *finally be completed.*

If I've failed to mention your name, the below is especially for you.
[Insert your name below…]

Finally, I would like to express a gratitude to _____, as she is truly a special part of my success! Thank you.

The Point of it All

I am upset with all you've gone through.
Oh, the innocent, headstrong, and **soul-shaking**—you.
If I could tell you and if you could see,
how angry and concerned—*why you **won't** listen to me*!
You need to understand that some things just are.
And some days you'll ask how'd you take it this far!
But one day he'll hurt, and you **will** run back …
And uncertainty and pain will push you off track.
And some days you'll cry and sometimes you'll fall.
And you will be overwhelmed, consuming it all!
'Cause years will just pass for love to submit,
and life and then love will just lust and then sit.
And you will walk though it—you can't get around!
And you will desert me, while facing the ground.
And I am so torn just watching you grow,
but I'll focus on the knowledge that someday you'll know.
I'll stop and I'll watch and wait 'til we peak,
'cause all that you've lived will help us to speak.
And all that experience—at such a short age!—
will help you and then me to create our next page …
and all of this madness will soon be fulfilled.
And all that we are—since we have been healed!—
it's all in our past—now seemingly small,
but I had to go through it—***it's the point of it all*** …

(A poem addressed to my teenage self)

Just for Me

I'm exactly where I'm supposed to be ...
to do what I'm supposed to do,
and learn what I'm supposed to learn,
in order to be who I'm supposed to be.
And in the end—what God has for me,
will be precisely what it's supposed to be—
just for me.

> ~ J.M. Tardy

Introduction

Girlfriend,

There is only one fact to this book, and everything else is my opinion. The fact is that there is nothing that you can do to keep your guy in a relationship, faithfully. There is not enough freakiness, intelligence, manipulation, or strength that can guarantee his commitment to you or your relationship. He must want it and that lifestyle for himself! Every single day he has to make a decision whether or not to remain loyal. Did you hear that? He has to make that soul-severing decision every day! When you can accept that secret, you are ready to see what he is really made of: his ingredient label.

That must be hard to digest, especially when everything else seems to be within your control. You've controlled your own destiny so far, right? You are holding down a job, you are mommy of the year, your house is in order, you've exceeded your every educational goal, and your girlfriends love you. But what about him? He is acting like he has lost his mind! He is the one crazy aspect of your life that you can't figure out. Welcome to reality! You've just realized the truth of the old adage that says you can't make a man stay where he doesn't want to be. Now what? Now you read this book.

Within these pages, I reveal honest situations that real women have experienced. I even share some of my own history and journal entries. I have to confess, it took me a long time to get to where I am today—in a happy and healthy relationship—but I'm sure glad I made it. Going through dozens of unhealthy relationships and billions of tears shed on unworthy men, I now have much to share. After interviewing dozens of women and standing face to face with my own truths, I can present our stories here. I've changed the names in order to keep the anonymity, but I'm sure you won't be as concerned with who these women are as with how they pushed through their situations. Each story is different, but valuable. I am sure that you will find yourself in at least one account.

The goal of this book is to give you a new perspective on dating and relationships. Dr. Wayne Dyer, author of *The Power of Intention*, said, "If you change the way you look at things, the things you look at will change." As with that quote, this book isn't meant to change your life; it is meant to change your perspective on dating and relationships so that you, too, can reach your level of "Zero Tolerance" for intolerable male behavior. This is a level that too few women attain, resulting in the continuance of a terrible cycle of damaging abuse, but I know that you can be stronger, and I look forward to hearing about your journey after you "arrive!" And in the end, please remember … it's okay and even necessary for us to take our time to get better.

God bless all of you who are my sisters in spirit. Allow yourself to be inspired and truly loved!

~J. M. Tardy

Today is the first day of the rest of my life. Who cares about the dates of when events happened? All I care about is that every event happened. Some events I may regret, but others I don't. Each one is a major or minor learning experience, depending on how I look at it. How I handle each one makes me who I am today. I don't know how I ever became fortunate enough to be me. I don't want to change anything major about myself and I consider that a blessing ...

~age seventeen

Chapter One:
Let's Go Shopping!

What if you had the luxury of literally shopping for your potential life partner? Walking from aisle to aisle or browsing a full-color print or online catalogue, wouldn't you take the time to carefully check out what each man is made of? Wouldn't life be easier if men could just wear ingredient labels?

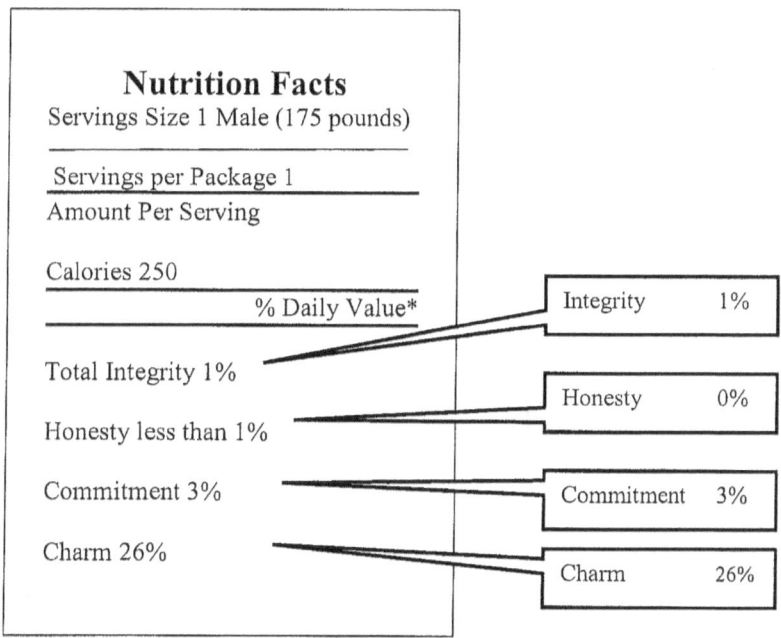

Nutrition Facts
Servings Size 1 Male (175 pounds)

Servings per Package 1
Amount Per Serving

Calories 250

% Daily Value*

Total Integrity 1%

Honesty less than 1%

Commitment 3%

Charm 26%

Integrity	1%
Honesty	0%
Commitment	3%
Charm	26%

If you were able to view this man's ingredient label, you would instantly know what your future with him held. You would have the discernment to understand that a man who has a low percentage of his character dedicated to honesty may be a liar. A man with a small percentage of commitment may be a cheater. A man who is average in charm may have "game." A man who is low in integrity might be ready to deceive. You could instantly conclude that you do not need his possible drama in your life. You would know that this man is more of a hassle than a helpmate. You would walk away and be satisfied with your decision. Right?

Unfortunately, men don't come with ingredient labels, and without them, understanding masculine components isn't a transparent process. It takes time, understanding, and discernment to fathom what a man is made of. Adult men are no longer those little boys made of "snips and snails and puppy dog tails," as the nursery rhyme used to tell us. As a matter of fact, the most challenging part of playing the dating game and investing in relationships is the ability to recognize the true character of a man in enough time to decide whether you should stay with him or move on without him.

Whether you are dating casually or in a committed relationship, there is the potential to absorb great hurt, anxiety, bitterness, pain, and insecurity. These are the toxins that we prefer to avoid in life; therefore, we need to be more aware of their proximity. How can one recognize those qualities in another person? I hear many women say, "I wish I knew then what I know now." The goal of this book is to help women in relationships learn to read their guy's ingredient label (i.e., interpret his character) in order to decide whether to pursue, be pursued, or walk away. Such knowledge will let you make a conscious and satisfying decision.

If you are a wife, girlfriend, "jump-off," mistress, "friend with benefits," or any other applicable term for a female that is involved with a male, then I am talking to you. Your relationship doesn't have to be sexual, it doesn't have to be formal, and it doesn't even have to be known or defined. Even if you feel that you are the only participant in your situation—girlfriend, you are still involved. Yes, you are "having relations" because you have allowed someone to occupy your time and impact your life. Keep reading, because the following is specifically for you.

Ingredient Labels

I don't know about you, but I have been on a healthy eating kick lately. I'm not sure what it is, but the older I get, the more my body starts to crave nutritious items like vegetables, fruits, and water—*I crave water*! I remember when I was in high school and college; I could eat anything and as much of it as I wanted with no side effects. I can't do that these days! Everything I eat that is unhealthy will stick right to my stomach and thighs. If I even daydream about donuts, I'm convinced that I will gain a pound or two.

So, I am cleansing myself. Of course, every now and again, I slip off the high road and eat something fatty or sweetened, but I eventually go back to my healthy regime, buying nutritional foods and sticking to sensible servings. Now, to manage this, I have to start paying more attention to the ingredients in foods. I can't just put anything into my body that smells good or looks tempting. I had to learn what was healthy and unhealthy for me, and why. It was not enough for someone to tell me to stay away from a Snickers Bar; I needed a reason. Yes, a Snickers Bar is so tasty that I have to know why I shouldn't eat one every day. The same principle applied to carbs, starches, and unwholesome fats. I couldn't just plunge into any kind of food I wanted. No, I had to seriously consider the effect of those foods on my body, my mind, and even my overall health and life. No matter how wonderful that hot fudge sundae (with double hot fudge) looked on the Dairy Queen sign, I couldn't just order one without thinking about the consequences. So if I ate that hot fudge sundae, I would have to skip breakfast or lunch—or both—to compensate for the calorie overload that was impacting my poor, unsuspecting figure.

Then, out of the blue, I began thinking about how to apply this same concept to men. Allow me to explain …

Like food, men (and women, for that matter) contain ingredients, but we use a different term for human ingredients. We call our additives "character." If you are trying to cleanse yourself from unhealthy relationships the way I cleansed my body from unhealthy foods, then maybe it is time for you to start reading men's ingredient labels. Character is defined as one of the attributes or features that make up and distinguish an individual. The character of a man is sometimes obvious, but at other times it is unclear. You have to understand a person and his behavior in order to identify character, just as you must be able to read an ingredient label in order to identify a product's composition. In either case, how would you ever know what you are about to ingest or invest in? Take a look at the matrix below.

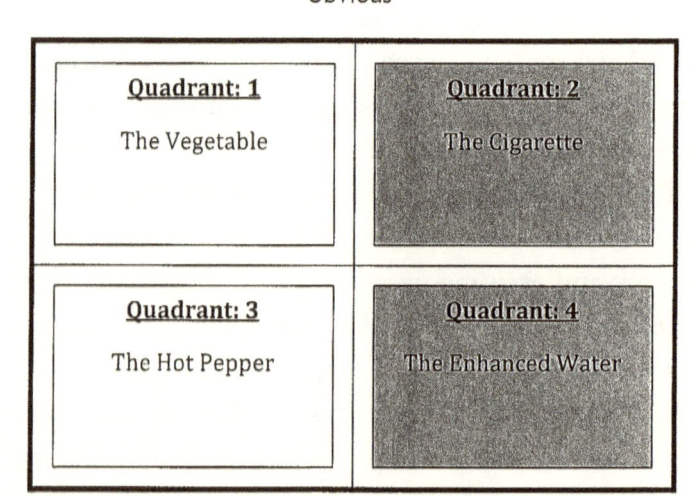

Obvious

Healthy		Unhealthy
Quadrant: 1 The Vegetable	**Quadrant: 2** The Cigarette	
Quadrant: 3 The Hot Pepper	**Quadrant: 4** The Enhanced Water	

Ambiguous

This matrix is divided into a clear zone and a shaded zone. The products within the clear zone (Quadrant One: the Vegetable, and Quadrant Three: the Hot Pepper) are healthier than those in the shaded zone. For example, most people know how good broccoli and beets are because studies have shown their positive effects on the body. But how many people actually know how healthy hot peppers can be for your body? Studies have shown the positive effects of hot peppers on health due to the capsaicin they contain. You may have heard of capsaicin because it can be found in over-the-counter pain relievers. Capsaicin in your diet can help to prevent heart disease by lowering cholesterol levels and blood pressure. And next to taking a capsaicin supplement, eating hot peppers, like cayenne peppers, is a great way to keep it in your diet. Who would have known? I didn't—*until I did a little research*!

Now, the products in the shaded zone (Quadrant Two: the Cigarette, and Quadrant Four: the Enhanced Water) are unhealthy. Need I take time to explain the negative side effects of cigarettes? I don't think so. You already know tobacco is harmful. You understand that the long-term side effects of smoking outweigh the short-term pleasures of nicotine. The bottom line is that you do not have to read the ingredient label of a cigarette package in order to know that smoking is unhealthy.

Now, pay attention to this one closely, because it's the most complex of the other three quadrants. The pros and cons of enhanced waters (i.e., SoBe Lifewater, or Glaceau Vitaminwater) are not as clear. Someone like me sees a tasty and refreshing water that happens to be enhanced with vitamins and believes that it could be a valuable addition to my daily eating plan. I instantly believe that I am going to enjoy the best of both worlds of taste and nutrition. I don't mind drinking water, since I'm starting to crave it more, and now I don't have to worry about remembering to take any vitamins. The nutrients are already in the water, right? How great is life? But there is one problem. Enhanced waters contain sugar. I mean loads of sugar! Some actually refer to these waters as sugar water. Studies have shown that enhanced waters can have as much sugar as a can of soda, like Coca-Cola or Pepsi. How can it be that most consumers aren't aware of this? This is because these waters are packaged so well that most consumers, like me, don't feel that they even need to check the ingredient labels, *but I am glad that I did.*

After my careful comparison of men to nutrients, I broke down the matrix further. The products in the top row are common knowledge to consumers. Without having to read an ingredient label, consumers have a general understanding of whether these items are good or bad for a person, whereas the products on the bottom row are more ambiguous. In order to really understand their positive or negative value, the ingredient label must be read closely. Taking time to learn what is inside an unknown food or beverage can mean the difference between being healthy or unhealthy.

As women, if you've been dating long enough, you've gone out with at least one guy from one of these representative quadrants. So have my girlfriends and I. Let's begin with the first row. The most obvious nutritional contrasts are Quadrant One: the Vegetable, and Quadrant Two: the Cigarette.

Angie landed in Quadrant One, the Vegetable, when she met Darrin. Darrin was a single, tall, dark brother. He didn't have a lot of money, but he handled his finances very well. Angie was impressed. As a high school teacher, he loved educating teenagers, and he wasn't looking to expand his career much further. He was degreed, polished, and polite. Doesn't he sound like a great catch?

He was. Darrin was a bona fide vegetable. He was everything that we are told as young girls to pursue in a prospective mate when we get older. But if we are not prepared to select a healthy vegetable, we sometimes find that we are not as impressed by him once we recognize that there is no edge to this guy that can compensate for our sweet tooth. This is what happened with Angie and Darrin. Now, Darrin was a fantastic catch to the average woman, but he wasn't adequate for Angie. He just wasn't aggressive enough. He was always by her side when she needed his time, but she didn't care to return the favor. Everything they did, like go to dinner, talk on the phone, and go to the movies, had to be on her terms. But Angie knew Darrin's worth; she knew that he was a good man (a vegetable) and held on to him. She would have been crazy to let him go. So she maintained the status quo with Darrin. In the meantime, she kept him holding on to a dream of what might be between them in the future while she continued to date others.

Toni planted her roots in Quadrant Two, the Cigarette, when she met Doug. Despite others' concerns, Doug seemed to be everything that Toni thought she was looking for. As long as I have known her, she has loved this man who is no good for her. Doug used to cheat, lie, and outright misuse Toni, but she is used to him by now. Moreover, Toni pursues men who are "no good" in general. She feels they need her, and she loves to give, give, and give. It has become an emotional crutch that she cannot let go of. Like Toni, we sometimes become addicted to the Cigarette— flaming, fiery, and exciting—but then, just a butt in the end.

Now, I believe that people stumble into Quadrant Three, the Hot Pepper, just like you find yourself in the grocery store's junk food aisle without planning it, but still come across your favorite low calorie snack bar and throw it in the basket. Jasmine did something like this when she met Tyler. What's funny is that she didn't meet him first; her girlfriend Samantha did. The day Samantha met Tyler she didn't think he was her type. See, Tyler was a waiter, and Samantha made six figures employed in corporate America. "Who dates a waiter?" Samantha asked me. Through small talk Samantha and Jasmine also realized that Tyler was a divorced single father of a little girl named Alicia. Samantha assumed Tyler had too much baggage, and he was just too low on the social scale for her to date seriously. So, Jasmine decided to date Tyler. Sadly, Samantha allowed Tyler to slip right through her fingers and into Jasmine's grasp. And now Jasmine is in love with a man who is intelligent, charming, honest, reliable, financially secure, and everything else she respects in a partner. Yes, Jasmine is in love with Tyler, and he loves her right back. And herein lies the twist to the Hot Pepper. From the outside, Tyler doesn't seem to have a lot to offer, but what Samantha didn't know is that Tyler owned the franchise where he was waiting tables. He is the best kind of father and example to his little girl. He isn't afraid of commitment, which is why he was married before. He believes in monogamy; the divorce came about because his ex-wife cheated on numerous occasions. And what about Samantha? Samantha is still single and looking for a Cigarette or a Vegetable—they're all looking pretty good these days, no matter which quadrant they hail from.

Now remember, men who fall into Quadrant Four, the Enhanced Water, are packaged so well with their charm, intelligence, style, and swagger that you forget to check that ingredient label. But when you do, you find they are no good for you, either.

Sherri fell for James in Quadrant Four. James was a poster child for Enhanced Water. James told Sherri everything she wanted to hear, and his actions showed her even more flattering responses. James wasn't the best-looking guy on the block, but his other qualities made him that much more appealing: He was extremely smart, and he had recently earned a Ph.D. and landed a great job. He treated Sherri so well that she was sure she was dating a man in Quadrant One: the Vegetable—*the clear zone.* James was good to her and for her. He was dependable, and Sherri never had to worry that he was cheating, lying, or manipulating her, nor was she concerned with other petty drama-related issues. He didn't bring those her way—until one day when James decided to take a vacation with some friends. They traveled to a Caribbean island where James met a woman who saw the same ingredients in him that Sherri had seen. For the first time in James' life, there were two women simultaneously interested in his nerdy yet successful persona. And for the first time, James had to make a decision. Unfortunately, even though Sherri had been by his side for a long time, the Caribbean woman was newer and quite interesting. In the end, he chose Miss Caribbean…

The scary thing about dating in the Enhanced Water category is that you are left feeling deceived. The interesting thing is that most of them don't realize they are deceiving you. The guy who falls into this quadrant is most likely to wake up one day and realize that his feelings for you or the relationship aren't as real as he once thought they were. Then he is stuck—

Health Kick Sidebar:

I believe one woman can be a good match and find satisfaction with many different men. I don't feel that there is only one person on earth for each of us. I don't believe in soul mates, per se. So I advise you to keep your eyes open and—go shopping! Don't settle for the first guy you meet, but don't wait around forever for Mr. Perfect, because he doesn't exist.

and so are you. Does he stay with you to not hurt your feelings, or does he leave you once he realizes the romance meter is no longer working? And there you have the dilemma of the Enhanced Water. By the end of the relationship, you are not sure if you are more upset that he led you on for so long or because his arriving at the truth changed all of the plans you both had made for the future.

The logical deduction from our discussion is that every man (and woman, for that matter) has an ingredient label. When you are "shopping" for a potential mate, you should be aware of which group you are dating in: Quadrant One (the Vegetable), Quadrant Two (the Cigarette), Quadrant Three (the Hot Pepper), or Quadrant Four (the Enhanced Water). It doesn't matter which quadrant you are exploring, but understand that there are pluses and minuses to each. Ask yourself which is most compatible with what you are seeking for the future. Then review which quadrant you have been dating in so far. How has that been working for you? Answers to these questions may help to reshape your shopping list.

I've learned that not everything in life that I want will I gain. There are some things in life that I have to accept. I may have to accept that [he] and I shouldn't be in a relationship. Maybe it is not the best thing for us. He shows me no respect. He expects me to do everything for him the way he wants it done. I have to leave him alone. The game gets me in relationships, but I believe that pride keeps me in one. Everyone kept saying that he and I wouldn't make it. I wanted to prove everyone wrong.

-age eighteen

Chapter Two:

Wait—Am I Ready for This?

Sometimes when you go shopping you find a new, exotic food on display. Maybe it's a spice you've never tasted before, or a special cut of meat not usually offered at this store. You decide to take a chance and buy it. Yes, it's out of your price range, and maybe it won't taste as good as it looks, but you're willing to try anything once, right?

This was Toni's personal motto. Remember Toni? Let me give you a little background on her and Doug. Now, Toni is a sharp woman. She could do a balancing act in her sleep. She is also a woman who married when she was fairly young. But that relationship did not work out, and she divorced within the next two years, retaining primary custody of a small daughter to care for. Toni continued her college studies and graduated on time, except she had to balance the responsibilities of raising a child, holding a job, attending school, and surviving a divorce all by herself. Handling these challenges would be difficult for a more experienced and mature woman, but Toni was still quite young. I admired her ambition; everyone did. No one worked harder or was more successful in all that she did than Toni.

But, like all of us, Toni had her own personal problems. Her weakness was choosing the wrong kind of men as her romantic interests. You see, Toni liked thugs or men who are rough around the edges. She was inherently attracted to men who, like hot peppers, offer a delicious edge and potential pain relief, but unfortunately, the latter never materialized. Some ladies cannot keep from gravitating toward men who are hard on women and weak on ambition; in fact, most of these men were inferior to Toni in key ways. Oddly, however, she enjoyed taking care of them, perhaps fulfilling her desire for a complete family or to have a companion in her life. This unequal pairing approach seemed to work for her, until she met Doug.

Toni confessed that Doug was no good, but she promised all of us, her concerned friends and family members, that she was wise to him and that she knew what she was doing.

"I'm just going to hang out with him to have something to do when I'm lonely; it's not serious," she reassured us.

Doug was not a long-term guy and definitely not the best role model for children. Having grown up in the streets with an ex-con father and a drug-abusing mother, Doug had received little guidance at home, and had few positive male role models to teach him how to treat women. Oh, he loved the ladies, all right, but he took what he wanted and left when he found something better. Doug was the classic user and abuser, the type of man that should be avoided at all costs. He seemed incapable of telling the truth. Doug learned to hide his emotions and actions from everyone, especially those with whom he had a relationship. He had learned early in life that it was painful to be accountable. The one time he had admitted to Toni that he had gone out with a female fitness trainer at the gym where he worked out, she had become angry and demanded that he never see the woman again, even though it had just been a casual beer or two at the bar. Doug's original impression of the world was thus confirmed: Never tell the truth, so you can't be held accountable or hurt other people. Toni, however, felt she was being fair and honest in laying out the "rules" for their relationship. She knew that Doug's background predisposed him to questionable actions and constant lying. So Toni's game plan was to play Doug before he played her. She would be the one calling the shots to make sure he didn't get the best of her.

But Doug was not new to this; he used Toni from the beginning. When the truth came out in a verbally abusive fight that the neighbors could overhear, he was still living with his ex-girlfriend and seeing Toni on the side, although she thought he was working extra hours that limited their time together. When Toni would drop by his house at the address he had given her, Doug would come out and meet her at the curb, saying he lived with his mother and didn't want their visit to intrude on their family time. Toni accepted this rather lame explanation, although she must have known it was a lie. Challenging him one night over a pile of accumulated evidence, she forced Doug to admit he actually had five children with five different women, although he had previously told her he had two children. Doug had lied to Toni continuously, and left the poor woman at home alone while he was out enjoying his life with friends and numerous other girlfriends, dodging child support and running into trouble with the law.

Even when the truth came out, as truth will, Toni continued to date him. I bet you are asking yourself, "Why in the world did she continue seeing this guy?" In other words, why make salad with a rotten tomato when, with a little bit of effort, you can buy a fresh one? Toni had clearly shopped for a man in the wrong ingredient quadrant, sort of like picking up a leftover item in the produce department's bargain bin. Why compromise her standards now?

I asked the same questions. You see, Toni was still determined to prove that the ball was in her court and that she was in control of what was happening in her relationship. But the truth was that, although she didn't expect much of Doug and was willing to settle for little, he didn't even meet her low expectations. Remember, the one thing that she expected was quality time with her man. When I asked her why she stayed in this unbalanced relationship for almost two years, she confessed that she loved Doug. Even though she had learned the truth about him early in the relationship, in her eyes the truth didn't matter because it was too late: Her feelings were deeply involved, and it was impossible to let go of him at that juncture in her life.

Toni started lying to herself the moment she met Doug, saying that she was only using him, when in reality she wanted a committed relationship and hoped their being together would move in that direction. Most women are looking for security and trust in a personal relationship, although Toni sensed Doug was not the kind of man to provide those things. She lied to herself repeatedly when she said that she was fine with her decision to stay with Doug, even after finding out that he had been lying to her since the beginning over the important aspects of his life: job, family, and responsibility. She tried to mislead me when she said that she was doing just fine, but I knew better. All of her close friends knew what was happening, and we felt sorry for Toni. She was a wonderful woman pouring her unique talents into a relationship that didn't really exist, and building a cocoon of dependence around a man who cared nothing about her. Even if Doug had anything to offer, he didn't give it to Toni—at least nothing of substance. But sadly, Toni settled for the crumbs leftover from his "other life," the time spent with rowdy friends and loose women when he completely closed her out and was blind to her relational needs. Instead, she should have shopped and expected only the finest ingredients for her relationship.

Of course, the pressure of maintaining the relationship is on Toni (and other women in her situation) because the "bad guys" aren't that invested or even that interested in keeping it going; there are always plenty of insecure women to hook up with. So it falls on the woman to make things work, even when it is crystal clear to everyone else that the situation is never going to pan out and certainly is not serving her best interests.

When a woman is in denial, she is insincere with herself. So she has no problem with trying to deceive you as her girlfriend. Sometimes she has lied so well to herself that she starts to believe her words to be truth. Like Toni, she desperately wants and needs to believe that her man cares as deeply for her as she does for him, and that he plans to change. She also believes that she will be the one to help him open up and express his feelings, as well as learn to treat her the way she feels she deserves. Many women are dominated by a strong savior complex

Health Kick Sidebar:

I believe that reality is the toughest world to live in, and not all of us are prepared to step into it. In order for you to comprehend the concept of his ingredient label, you must first be able to recognize when he is revealing himself to you. You can't see what he is made of if you are lying to yourself or living in a fantasy world far removed from where he lives. If you are this kind of woman, this may not be the time to read this book. Hold on to it— but wait a while.

or maternal instincts; they long to save a man from the path of destruction. But too often, she finds herself pulled along his trek to the underworld and unable to escape his magnetic charms or web of deceit. However her scenario plays out, she isn't trying to hear what you have to say about her relationship or her man. She wants to view the dinner salad she has just set on the table as wholesome, crisp, and delicious, when in actuality the lettuce is wilted, the tomatoes are rotten, and the croutons are stale. Toni had settled for second-rate—or even third-rate—ingredients in her man when she could have had top shelf.

A woman in denial may be so because she feels the person she's dating has potential. She remembers the way things used to be with her man, or the way he has promised her things will be in the future. She longs for a secure, nurturing, stable relationship with a partner who cares as deeply about her as she does for him. But she values herself too little to have any serious chance of finding the happiness she is seeking. This is the kind of woman who stays with her man because she knows what he will be once … (fill in the blank). Or she is still living off the vision of what he used to be when they first started dating. These women say things like, "I don't know what to do anymore," "I am not making excuses for him," "He is not the best guy, but …" "He isn't treating me good right now, but …" "He used to …" and "I know what he can be if he would just …" We, her caring friends, would finish those statements in quite a different way than she would, but let's face it, we are talking a foreign language when we try to encourage and advise our girlfriends against settling for substandard treatment.

Toni, wise and talented in many important ways, allowed herself to be manipulated and deceived by a man who was little more than a con artist. Smart enough to know the truth, she interpreted the facts in a gentler version to allow herself to save face by staying with Doug. As their so-called relationship dragged on, however, it became increasingly evident to Toni that the facts could only be truly interpreted one way, and that was to reveal that Doug was using her in a highly degrading manner and deserved no place in her life. Like moldy produce and expired salad dressing, Doug should have been discarded long before.

The moral of the story is that the hardest woman to try and talk sense to is the one who is in denial. As a matter of fact, I don't even speak to those women; I just listen. You cannot help a woman who refuses to be realistic about her situation. These women don't want anyone's opinion or help; they simply want someone to vent to when necessary, so they can calm down enough to keep the relationship (if it can be called that) going indefinitely. And at the end of the day, that it is their business and I can respect that.

Once again, here I am just sitting, plotting, planning and waiting to get some time with [him]. I don't even want him. It's just very important to me that he wants me!

~ten days before my twentieth birthday

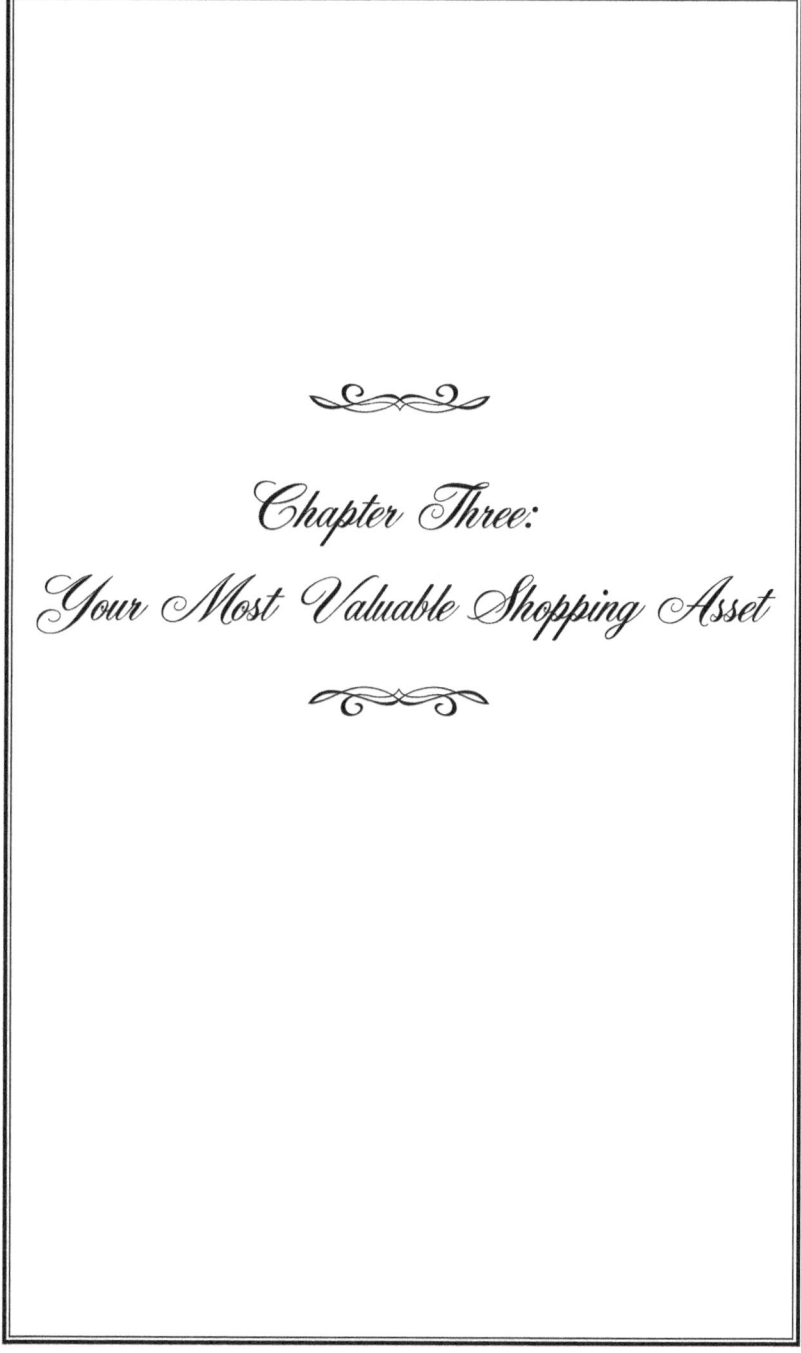

Chapter Three:

Your Most Valuable Shopping Asset

Have you ever wandered down the grocery store aisle, following your carefully prepared shopping list, when all of a sudden, you find out the item you were seeking was out of stock? Well, let me ask you, if you can't find just what you want, do you make a substitution or wait patiently until next week when they restock the item you are seeking? "It depends," would be my answer. For me, it depends on if this item is worth it. Is it worth the time that I'll have to go without? If yes, then I'll wait. If no—substitution, it is!

Let me introduce you to April. April was a relationship shopper who settled for second-rate ingredients. She, in many ways, was much different than Toni, although they seemed to share one thing in common: both were lonely. Unlike Toni, April appeared to be fighting several deep personal issues from the day we met. She was not as confident about herself or her abilities, nor was she as independent as Toni. Somewhat insecure, April is what I would consider to be a passive-aggressive woman. She was a spoiled child who grew into an even more spoiled and self-centered woman. April didn't have to ask for much in life, whether it was clothing, spending money, or fun things to do, because everything was handed to her by parents who were more interested in April's happiness than her well-being. April did not have much experience in shopping for the better bargains in the male department. In fact, she typically shopped without considering the blend of ingredients or the wholesomeness (or lack thereof) in the men who interested her. April could have made a more suitable selection of date-mate if she had been less preoccupied with immediate self-gratification and, instead, had spent more time thinking about the reciprocal aspects of a healthy relationship. After all, you don't go grocery shopping and buy shellfish when you are allergic to it. Sure, those little shrimps, clams, and lobsters taste great going down, but later you are going to pay big time. Unfortunately, April isn't the kind of woman to accept unsolicited advice. She shopped extravagantly and carelessly, failing to read the tiny print on her men's ingredient labels.

When I met her, she had just reentered the dating market after an unfortunate relationship that had failed, in part, due to April's disinterest in taking responsibility for her actions and facilitating an evenhanded give-and-take approach with her man. The breakup was bitter, though April was used to shrugging off what she considered superficial pain, and she expected others to do the same. Had she taken some time to reflect on what had gone wrong and apply that self-knowledge to personal growth and relational sensitivity, she might have avoided her next relationship mistakes.

After the emotional fallout with her ex-boyfriend had settled somewhat, April's life went on as usual. She didn't realize that she was ready to start dating again until Lucas approached her. That was just like April: She didn't even have to go "shopping" for her new man; he came to her instead. She called to tell me that she had met a wonderful guy. She said that she realized instantly that this man was not what she needed in her life, due to his unstable history and questionable future. Did you hear that? She confessed that she knew he probably wasn't what she needed. According to April, Lucas was thirty-eight, worked a third-shift entry-level job, had three children by three women, and, in her opinion, he had "issues." The only thing she liked about Lucas was his humor; far from uptight and boring, Lucas was able to lighten daily stress from their jobs and bring amusement to her life through jokes, games, and teasing. He knew how to laugh and have fun—and April desperately wanted a good time in her life. In fact, Lucas demonstrated many ways of ignoring life's problems and sidestepping responsibility, and these qualities immediately attracted April, who had spent much of her life avoiding the same things. Good humor was the only thing that kept Lucas in the picture. If it weren't for that, he would never have stood a chance with April.

That explanation for their magnetic attraction seems simple and innocent enough, right? It's funny, but April never even knew what hit her the moment Lucas came into her life. In the beginning, in response to his easygoing nature, she felt in complete control of the relationship as long as she was laughing. She vowed that nothing would go wrong in her relationship with Lucas, because she knew that upsets or problems would lead the couple down a rough road of drama. April's loneliness and longing to connect with someone who made her feel good allowed her to give Lucas a portion of her time. That's it. Period! According to April, nothing more was going to happen. Her plan was "foolproof."

When she and I discussed this growing relationship, I faced one of those difficult situations where a friend hesitates to offer a negative opinion because in our case, I was happy that she was happy again. It's like when a dear friend who's allergic to shellfish throws caution to the wind at a party and overindulges—you want to warn her, but somehow you just can't bring yourself to interrupt her joyous appreciation of the seafood specialties. But when the hives appear and her stomach acts up, you feel guilty for not speaking up. The same was true for her relationships; we, her friends, wanted April to be happy, so we tried not to dampen her enthusiasm when guys almost literally showed up at her door—a special delivery, you might say. And who can turn down a load of groceries brought right to your doorstep? Who's going to pause and read the ingredients before digging in?

April had been through some bad times, and I was glad she had gotten over the pain of her failed relationship. I knew that she needed some good humor in her life, especially since, although she had healed from the break, April remained frustrated from the outcome of her prior relationship. The interesting thing is that she asked my opinion regarding her budding romance with Lucas. I told her three things that she remembers to this day.

First, I told her she needed to decide for herself how far she really wanted this union to go instead of just accepting the "anything is possible" mentality.

Second, I warned her to pay more attention to Lucas' character beyond the fact that he was funny. For example, April should observe him in a variety of interactions to find out if he was sensitive, generous, kind, tolerant, trustworthy, and understanding— instrumental qualities in a meaningful relationship. After all, Lucas had been able to create enough trust with three women in order to bear children with them and yet had lacked the necessary qualities to sustain a relationship with any of them!

Finally, I warned her to "wrap it up." She obviously was with a super-fertile man and needed to take extra precautions. That man had some scary ingredient additives! But she called me three weeks later saying she was in love. She called me six months later, saying she couldn't trust him anymore. She called me one year later saying she was pregnant. Isn't it amazing how much life can happen in such a small amount of time?

Girlfriend to girlfriend, I want to let you in on a huge secret. This secret, when I heard it, changed my life. How could I have been so ignorant before? When I was in college, I dedicated too much time to this one particular guy, but that is a story we will delve into in a later chapter. He and I used to share a lot of deep but random conversations. Each conversation would start off with an introspective question like, "Do you know the meaning of serendipity?" He would then pull out the dictionary and suggest that I look it up, because if I learned the definition myself, I would never forget it. And then the conversation would build from there. One particular day we were sitting and talking, and he asked, "What is your most valuable asset?" He gave me a second to reflect on his question, and then he asked again: "What is your most valuable asset?"

I felt ridiculous because I thought that I could answer his question effortlessly. I said,

"My body. My body is my most valuable asset!"

Now I know you must be thinking: "Your body?" But I was only seventeen or eighteen and I really didn't give the matter much thought.

He said, "You're wrong! Think about it again."

I said, "Sex?"

He said, "No, your most valuable asset is time."

It's been so long since he passed this wisdom on to me, which his father had passed on to him, but I still remember it as though it were yesterday. Over the years, I've had plenty of time to reflect on this notion of time being my most valuable asset. Think of it another way. Time is so important that nothing can happen until it is given away—whether voluntarily or involuntarily. Consider the many activities that you cannot participate in until your time is given away: dating, working, loving, sex, etc. Once you give away time, you can never get it back, so be careful who you share it with and how you spend it. That was—and is—the lesson. This was the most valuable advice I have ever received, and now I am sharing it with you. Do you see how dating works now? It's not about the money we spend on each other, although that can play a significant role. More importantly, it's the amount of time—and its quality, or lack thereof—that determines our attitude toward a relationship and the likelihood of its success.

Like many women, April has frivolously thrown time away to people who are undeserving. Like crumbs of stale bread, she scatters her minutes and hours in a path that she hopes will lead to her longed-for happiness with Luke, but this crazy couple keeps ending up being more lost and in greater danger together than they were apart.

How many of your girlfriends allow men or women in their lives that they know misuse their time? Think back for a second to April. She clearly stated that Lucas was not deserving of her time, but she shared much of it with him. Her occasional hours grew into weeks and months, and then a year. That investment of time is all that was needed to create a lifetime of guilt, disappointment, and frustration. Some of you know how it is; you buy up a huge supply of sale chocolate at the store and wolf it down, only to repent over the days, weeks, or months that follow as you try desperately to shed those unwanted extra pounds. Emotional baggage from a careless relationship can lead to similar regrets afterward. That is why it is critical to read those ingredient labels carefully, ladies!

What about you? I bet you can think of some women who have let their hours trickle away like pennies falling into a wishing well. Be sure that the people in your inner circle value your time as much as you value theirs. Remember that each day is an investment in the people around you, and the more you invest, the harder it becomes to walk away. Ensure that the person receiving your time actually deserves every second that he is given. I can hear you asking, "But how would I know if he didn't deserve my time?"

Keep reading—I'll tell you in the next chapter!

Health Kick Sidebar:

We talk about how we don't have time for drama in our lives. I am a firm believer that you should keep this same rule of thumb for your family, friends, and associates. If you don't have time for drama, allow your actions to demonstrate this!

At times, I wish I had never met [him] because I could have saved so much of me. He has never been there for me, and I'm always making excuses for him. I'm fed up with all of this! He never spends time with me. He never calls to check up on me. He never keeps his word, and he is still messing with other women. He does not even have enough respect to just date me and no one else. I just don't understand him. I deserve better than this kind of guy—I know I do. So why do I stay? Why is he on his way over here now? Maybe it's because I just don't care anymore. I don't care if he comes or goes. I don't care if he calls me back or not. I don't feel anything for him so now I want to see if I feel anything with him.

~age twenty

Chapter Four:

Hiccups

Do you ever get carried away in the bakery of the grocery store when you spot a moist red velvet or double milk chocolate cake on display? Your mouth just waters, doesn't it? Suddenly, without thought or plan, you have to buy that cake! At home you serve it with your delicious meat and side dishes, and then you eat your fill and more, realizing belatedly that you have overdone it. Just after eating, a case of hiccups set in, ruining that wonderful after-dinner glow that follows a truly special meal.

Hiccup!

Hiccup, hiccup!

They won't stop. Why didn't you chew more slowly or eat less?

Of course, even a well-planned meal can lead to a bit of indigestion. Sometimes a slight burp or hiccup means that the meal was highly satisfying and simply needs to be more fully digested. But at other times a signal of this type may be telling you to stay away from a particular food or seasoning, as it does not agree with your body.

Sometimes hiccups develop when people get over excited or have eaten too much. Have you ever noticed how a hiccup can throw off the consistency in your breathing? Getting an unexpected case of the hiccups can interfere with a speech, an important conversation, or even basic concentration when you are trying to get something done. It has been documented that hiccups may be the result of too much oxygen in the body. This causes the diaphragm to contract to keep you from taking in even more oxygen. These contractions are the hiccups. For most of us, hiccups can be uncomfortable, embarrassing, and just plain obnoxious. All you want to do is get past a hiccup so your breathing can return to normal and ordinary life can continue.

A healthy relationship can be synonymous with your lungs' normal performance. Just as your lungs contract and expand appropriately, promoting the proper flow of oxygen throughout your body's organs and cells, your relationship progresses normally. A relationship often advances as expected, with both persons performing their roles to maintain the connection, just as lungs pump air through the torso and limbs to maintain oxygen flow. Suddenly, something changes, whether your guy is not engaged the way he usually is, not as responsive as he usually is, or begins to act differently, perhaps by emotionally withdrawing or becoming less available. This is the hiccup in the relationship, interrupting your life together just as a physical hiccup disrupts the smooth distribution of oxygen by the lungs. I'm sure most of us have gone through a hiccup episode and can relate to these descriptions. Something changes in your relationship, and the balance between partners becomes skewed. You feel disconnected, ill at ease, and out of rhythm. On a physical level, all you want to do is go and find that glass of water to drink, hold your breath, or breathe into that brown paper bag in order to get rid of your hiccup. Unfortunately, with relationships, it may not be as simple as that. There is no easy remedy to restore balance and order between the two of you. A relational hiccup requires serious thoughtful reflection and possible adjustments.

Let's go back to Toni's story for a moment. When Toni met Doug, both were content in the relationship as it commenced, and Toni felt that she was the one using Doug, just for someone to spend time with. But then came an unexpected hiccup. Doug stopped calling the way he used to. He became more lax in checking in with her and in spending time with her. From Toni's perspective, these changes seemed to occur out of the blue. Why did Doug stop being responsive?

I am a firm believer that hiccups typically have something to do with a distraction. Something (or someone, for that matter) has distracted your man, and if you want your oxygen intake back on track, it is your job (more than that, it is your duty) to find out what that distraction is—immediately! The wrinkle in the relationship may be due to your man going through personal problems, like jumbled finances or an argument with a family member, so that he can't really focus on you at the moment. Or he may be dealing with something more troubling to the relationship, such as the distraction of another woman. Your goal is to acknowledge that you are going through a relational hiccup, determine its cause, and work it out as needed. There are many, many ways to predict an occurrence of hiccups or to know if you are experiencing hiccups right now. Following are ten of the most common ways to tell if you may have an episode coming on.

Aware of his intentions

Do you remember my girlfriend Angie, who was not impressed with Darrin, the Vegetable? While she was dating Darrin, she met Jamel. Now, Jamel didn't want to come on too strong in the beginning, so instead of asking for Angie's number, he mentioned that he was on Facebook, and invited her to check out his Web site and leave her contact information there if she felt comfortable enough to do so. Angie found it odd that he didn't ask for her number or e-mail address, but she was interested in this guy, and going to his Web site seemed like a safe option. Angie admitted that this really helped her to discover a lot about his background, his career goals, and even his favorite TV shows. This stimulated her interest in him because she discovered that they shared common interests and goals. For example, they loved the program *King of Queens*. So she decided to read a little further to determine if they were indeed as well matched as she suspected. One section asked a question that he answered in a way that Angie would never forget. The question was, "What do you like doing in your free time?" He answered with one word: "Women!" This guy had the nerve to put an exclamation point behind the word as emphasis. When she told me about this, I couldn't help but laugh. We gave him the nickname, "Mr. Doing Women," whenever we referred to Jamel. This one answer told Angie everything she needed to know. His favorite pastime is "doing" women, and he is arrogant enough to announce it to the world. It is safe to say that Angie did not pursue this guy.

Listen, ladies. When a man starts telling you about himself, you should listen. The most obvious way to know if a man will bring hiccups into your relationship eventually is because he has warned you that he will. You are a lucky woman to be able to hear a man say, "I don't want anything serious; I just want to chill for a while." If he says that he is not interested in a relationship or marriage, listen to him. The odds are that he means what he says. From there, it becomes your fault if you fall for this man, knowing that he has no intention of getting emotionally involved in you. If you decide to walk away from him, understand that his decision does not make him a bad person; it just means that he is not what you are looking for. This was true regarding "Mr. Doing Women." Angie and I neither thought nor joked that he was a bad person; she was just not interested in a man who *loves* pursuing women in his spare time. Feel blessed that he is handing over his ingredient label to you. All you have to do is read it, and it's not even in fine print.

Missing in action

Toni could never find Doug! I mean, she grew furious because the only time that Doug would call her was after 11 p.m. He started getting to the point where he would miss her calls all day, and then when it was time for him to rest his head, he would start blowing up her cell phone. He would become upset if she questioned him too much, especially when all he wanted to do was come and see her, as she had been begging all day. Can you relate to how Toni must have felt?

If you called your guy right at this moment, would he answer? Does the thought of calling him put knots in your stomach because you know that you will be speaking to his voice mail—again? Do you get this feeling in your gut that you won't hear from him until the weekend is over, until his friends are out of town, until he runs out of money, until something? Where is he—and why does he always have to call you back? The reality of the matter is that most men who aren't available most of the time aren't accessible because they do not want to be. There are twenty-four hours in a day. Could he really be that busy? Seriously, girlfriend—look at how busy you are each day. You still find time to check in with him, right? It doesn't matter what excuse he gives you; if he is consistently missing in action, remember that it is not by chance, it's by choice.

Quality time

Janelle would plan the most elaborate romantic nights for one guy she dated, Terrance. See, Terrance worked out of town as a traveling salesman. He only came home a few weekends a month. Janelle would go all out to make him feel like he was king of her earth. It was important to her that she got the music right, the Hennessy that she knew he loved, and the oils for his massage. I mean, she did more in her on-again, off-again relationship than most married women do for their husbands—but that, too, is another story. Terrance, on the other hand, had other priorities. It was the same routine every time he came home. He would spend a little time with his family and the majority of time with his friends, and then he would stumble into her place around 2 a.m. on the day he had to leave. Of course he would disrupt her sleep, but she would wake up and cater to him as usual. Janelle was like a nighttime binge eater; she knew it was bad for her, but she just couldn't seem to help herself. She indulged whenever the opportunity presented itself, failing to thoughtfully consider the consequences of consuming the unwholesome ingredients represented in Terrance. She could've waited for steak, but settled for baloney.

Most of us enjoy quality time with those we care about. Remember, when you give someone your time, you are giving him your most valuable asset because time, once spent, is gone forever. Knowing this, you often want to share your boyfriend's schedule, which signifies that he chooses to be with you above other friends and interests. There is nothing wrong with wanting some of his time, as most of us enjoy quality hours spent with loved ones. What's going on in your current relationship? Does your quality time with him come consistently after his friends have theirs? Please understand that it is okay for each of you to spend time alone. I am not saying that you have to be glued at the hip. The key is to spend the right amount of time together—*an amount both of find comfortable*. And remember, a guy will spend time with you if he wants to be with you. Or not.

Alone in your relationship

I used to work with Terry, a great employee and trustworthy friend. In her early forties, Terry was engaged to Will. This was to be her second marriage and also Will's second marriage, if he would ever sit down with Terry long enough to work on their wedding plans. Their engagement had been prolonged six years. Terry was tired of the delay. She no longer wanted to live alone, while Will was comfortable staying with his parents. Terry was tired of not having Will's companionship because he was always preoccupied with other priorities, such as his parents' lawn, his friends' football nights, and overtime at his job. Will still took care of Terry financially, but physically and emotionally, Terry was all alone, and she increasingly hated it. She and I went to lunch one day where we talked for a long time about how relationships should be. She confessed something I will never forget. She said the saddest feeling in the world is the sense of being alone in your relationship. She admitted that she was afraid to start dating anyone new at her age. She didn't think that she had the emotional strength. She would wait for Will to come around without really badgering him to do so. She lacked the courage and the conviction to move on without him. Rather than checking out his ingredients, she just tossed him in the cart with the goal of "making do," however he turned out.

The saddest emotion is feeling alone in your relationship! I bet some of you know this feeling all too well. He won't go anywhere with you. He isn't a phone person. He would rather spend his time away from you while doing whatever it is that makes him happy. Is it worth being in a relationship if you feel lonely? It isn't. You should feel a partnership developing with your significant other. You should be happy with or without that person around, but hopefully he is around a good part of the time. Although you should have a comfortable amount of space in any healthy relationship, this amount of "alone" time isn't healthy and over time will gradually kill any chance of happiness.

Cold feet

Toni's boyfriend, Doug, never planned for the future. He lived day to day by the seat of his pants. That was okay for Toni, so this scenario doesn't apply to her and doesn't apply to you if you are dating a guy like Doug. Now, Janelle, on the other hand, was in a relationship with Terrance, "the salesman." He hadn't always traveled or spent most of his time with friends. He used to be completely dazzled by Janelle. He would openly tell her things like how he could see her as the mother of his children. He could spend the rest of his life with her. They would talk about what their wedding could be like. Right around the time that she started noticing he didn't want to give her his quality time on the weekends, she also observed that he would become more distant when she reminisced about conversations regarding their future. He didn't want to talk about those hopes and dreams anymore. How could the mere mention of those previous romantic conversations now make him angry?

Has your guy started saying things like, "This is too much pressure," or, "I think we need to slow down because we are moving too fast?" Although these are not clear red-zone cases, they definitely should be watched closely. You should observe and analyze your actions, and his. This is a good time to introduce my ***Reasonable Person Theory***. Really think about what you have requested from him lately. Would a reasonable person consider your requests to be too much pressure or moving too quickly? If you answer "yes" to this question, then you may need to reevaluate your behavior in this relationship. If you answer "no," then you may be dating a man who has entered the shaded zone. Pay attention to the shaded zone, ladies. Is everything all of a sudden too much for him? Simple requests like asking him to show up on time, keep his word, or spend time with you are not unreasonable to a man who wants to be in a relationship. For him to feel pressure from these requests may be an indicator that something is not right. If the grocery item you are shopping for appears discolored, mislabeled, or has unusual markings that become visible as you examine it more closely, put it back on the shelf and keep looking for the ingredients that will better serve your purposes.

Poor decision-making

Have you ever given a guy *the look?* I mean, you gaze right into his eyes, your chin resting in the palm of your hand, with a slight smile on your face, as you say to yourself, "I wonder if this guy realizes that he will *never* see me again?" I can't be the only one who has given this look before, right? I'm sure you know what I mean. One of my co-workers was telling me about a date with a guy she met through a matchmaking service. She said that he discussed his concerns with electing a black president, with women being in high-powered positions instead of staying at home with their children, and his whole frustration with affirmative action programs. She admitted that she went along with the dinner while wearing a huge smile, but she knew that she would never see this man again. She confessed that she had given him "the look," too. Isn't that funny?

I feel that some decisions by the other person in a relationship demonstrate my priority in someone's life. I used to think it was clever to tell men that they were making bad decisions. This was almost as if to warn them that if they continued this behavior, I would simply walk away and they wouldn't hear from me again. But I don't do that anymore; I simply use "the look." Now, we all make bad decisions. Some may be non-issues over small, non-essential items, while others might be deal breakers for the relationship. It's up to each woman to decide what her threshold will be. For example, a guy who doesn't call you back as promised, in my opinion, is making a bad decision. This doesn't become a deal breaker for the relationship until he begins to do this consistently. In another instance, if the man that you are dating gets up and walks out in the middle of an argument, I deem that a bad decision that, if done consistently, can also be a deal breaker. Regardless of the zone you are in, bad decisions should be observed closely. Using our shopping analogy, this would be like finding a small bruise on a piece of fruit, and then examining the entire skin to be sure the fruit is truly edible, not bruised even more significantly under the skin or near the stem.

Checks and balances

I hate it when people hide things! The advent of many types of technology makes hiding things much easier. With cell phones, text messages, e-mails, voice mails, Facebook, MySpace, and so on, who can even keep up with all of the options, much less keep an eye on their use?

I joke with my girlfriends about this, but you must admit that it has truth. If your man watched you approach his cell phone, e-mail, backpack, or briefcase, how would he respond? Go up to him and touch his cell phone while he is looking directly at you. Open it. Does the thought of doing this make you nervous because you know that you will probably find something that you don't want to see? How many times has the thought of your being near his personal items caused arguments? Clearly, this is his personal space, and I would never tell you to go in search of information or to read his messages. The concept is not to play a game, but instead do what I call checking in with your man. If he has nothing to hide, he could care less what you do with his phone. If there is something iffy there, regardless of how small, you will recognize it in his expression. Clearly, this is the most immature activity on my list of recommendations, but I promise, it works every time. There are no secrets in a healthy relationship, right?

His friends

Effie told me about a time when she decided to hang out with Sean and his friends. Now, Effie and Sean had an interesting relationship because she could never really determine where she stood with him. Sean wanted to be in a relationship when he wanted to be, but he expected Effie to be his girlfriend at all times. That probably explains why she hadn't met his friends before and why she was excited when he finally extended the invitation. More than that, she was excited to be a part of whatever kept taking his time away from her. All of them agreed to go to a lounge to hang out. Effie was pleased to meet Sean's good-time buddies, but couldn't help but notice that every time Sean wasn't looking, one of his friends would flirt with her by smiling suggestively or making an intimate comment.

Remember this: You can tell how a man talks about you by paying attention to how his friends treat you. When he brings you around his buddies, are they trying to hit on you? Are they in your face the moment he walks out of the room? Maybe he doesn't even need to leave. Is it funny to him that they try to move in on you while he is there? Here are a few basic rules of thumb. How a man's friends treat you depicts how he has described you to them. No true friend of his would be so disrespectful as to hit on you the moment he leaves the room *or* while he is there. As a matter of fact, if your relationship were healthy, he would never bring you around those kinds of guys in the first place. Keep in mind the old adage that one rotten apple can spoil the whole barrel. So when shopping for a man, ladies, beware that the shiny one doesn't have a wormy spot [in spreading rumors about you] that will pollute the rest. Check out your guy's character carefully to avoid getting stuck with a bad bargain.

What he isn't saying

Toward the end of Janelle's relationship with Terrance, she could feel that something wasn't right. She could see that he was not communicating with her openly or honestly anymore. But what confirmed her doubts and suspicions was the day she kept asking him to come over for a heart-to-heart with her. You see, Janelle wanted to follow the relationship through to its conclusion, but she kept waiting for Terrance to end it. On one particular day, Janelle finally convinced Terrance to stop by and see her in the morning. He didn't seem excited to be there. He had the look of someone who had been made to feel guilty in order to get quality time. He sat down beside Janelle on her comfortable plush sofa, and he focused his attention on the floor, hardly saying a word. He knew that the "heart-to-heart" was about to start, and he was not in the mood for it. Janelle tried to ease the tension in the room by sliding her foot over to his leg. She softly rubbed her toe against his calf. The moment this happened, he brushed his leg away and got up from the sofa. Without saying a word, he walked out of the house, got into his car, and drove away.

Have you asked your man a direct question? I mean, have you asked him something that could answer it all? *Are you leaving me? Do you love her? Who is she? Where were you last night?* When you asked the question, did he dance around the answer? My favorite type of creative liar is the one who never answers. When the tension increases, he tries to argue his way out of the problem by making excuses, passing the blame, or changing the subject. What isn't he saying? Pay attention to that. This is a tough red flag to see because most of us are afraid to ask the tough questions. Even more importantly, most of us are afraid of how we will have to respond to the answer.

Sometimes you get in the mood for that delicious cream pie sold by the corner bakery. You've bought and enjoyed it on several occasions, but you notice the quality seems to be declining. The last few times it hasn't been as fresh, or there wasn't as much filling. Finally you try having a talk with the baker, only to get the runaround. The solution? It's obvious. Stop buying the pie and stay away from that bakery. As you can see, shopping for quality foods is very similar to finding the right man for a relationship.

Patterns in past relationships

I thought I was different when I started dating my best friend of eight years. Within our friendship, I watched him move a woman to another state with him after college, and then ask her to move back home three weeks later. I watched him back out of relationship after relationship when things started getting too serious. I was his best friend. He didn't have to tell me anything; I witnessed it. But for some reason, I still thought that I was different from his girlfriends, that being his closest confidante and pal

Health Kick Sidebar:

Another red flag that we must pay attention to is the cycle of attraction. We can continuously attract the same person over and over again. These men will keep approaching you time and time again, but each time with a different look, a different personality, different credentials, or even a different upbringing, but one thing remains the same: their ingredients. You will know if you fit in this category, because you keep going through the same issues over and over again. You keep looking for the same type of guy. Maybe the super-aggressive guy isn't what you really need right now, maybe it's not the thug, maybe it's not the NBA player. You must learn from this so that you are better able to recognize him the next time around, wherever you are and whoever he might be.

would somehow place me higher in his regard. However, I wasn't treated any better than the others. He did the same things to me when we decided to date seriously. At first we were completely fine with our long-distance relationship. We were in sync, we had fun together, and we trusted one another. I never would have guessed that he would begin having commitment problems with me. But he did, and they began the day that he and I moved to the same state. Within three weeks he was asking me to move out. In retrospect, I can't blame him. I can only blame myself. I had an advantage that other women didn't. I had been able to see his pattern in past relationships. Had I paid attention the way I should have, I wouldn't have found myself becoming a statistic as well.

What about you? If your man discussed his past relationships with you or you were able to be a part of his life before, then you are a lucky woman. How did he describe other women to you? What did he do in situations that may not have been favorable to him? Does he have a history of leaving women with little excuse and no warning? Do you see similar bad patterns emerging in your relationship with him? Although his past does not necessarily predict his future, it should be taken into consideration as part of his ingredient label.

In the end, remember that although hiccups may be a disruption, embarrassment, and/or inconvenience, they can be your best friend and save you many tears and sighs. They also can help you to see something that you may not have been able to notice before. Remember this: If a relationship is what he wants, then he needs to treat you accordingly. Do not be fooled. These men who dodge honesty and avoid communication are clearly signaling that they may not be interested in a serious relationship. If you want to be part of a couple that is mutually respectful and interested in moving forward, then the kind of man described above may not be the best choice for you. Any man who is interested in being part of your life for a long time will *not* do these things. Don't be fooled into believing that you have to settle because you believe all men are like this. All men are *not* like this. Remember, there are plenty of choices at the supermarket. Ditto for the dating market!

So many…so many times I found myself crying over [him]. I can swear to you that every time I cried it hurt like hell. If I had never met him, my life would be completely different, but now my life will never be the same.

~age twenty

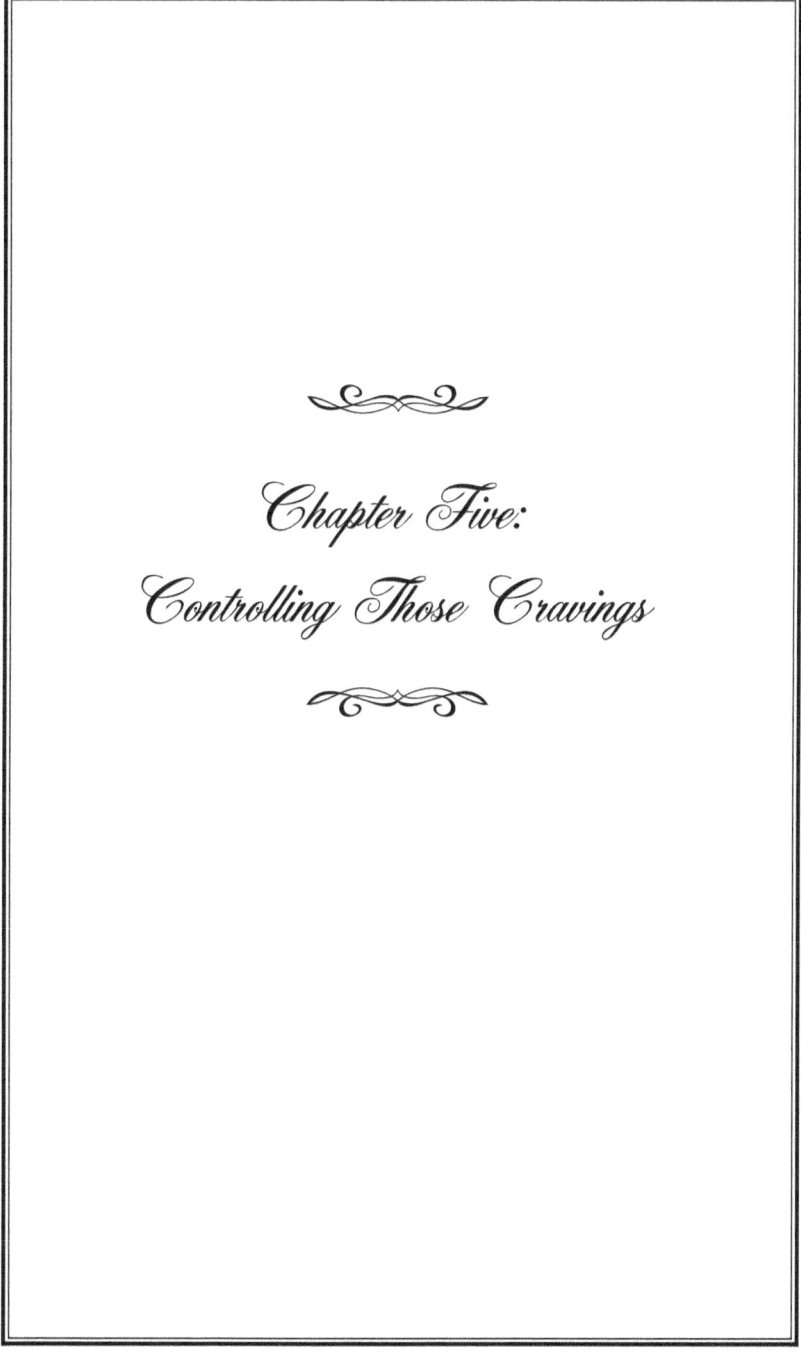

Chapter Five:

Controlling Those Cravings

Cravings can be so hard to control sometimes! I fight against my sweet tooth all the time. Sometimes those cravings can be so strong that all I want to do is dive into a tub of muffins and stay there for the rest of the day and I don't care who knows it. At that moment, I could care less about what muffins are made of and how eating all of that sugar can ruin my health kick. The same is true in relationships. We can become so overcome by our own emotions and passions that we begin allowing them to control the decisions we make. Take a look at Janelle's case below.

Emotional versus rational

Janelle has a much softer demeanor than any of the other girls I've met. She is quieter and more reserved. Janelle has to know you before opening up, and even once she lets you into her circle, she remains a relatively composed and somewhat inaccessible woman.

Janelle bases some of her biggest decisions on emotions. She drives me crazy with that. I can't tell you the number of times she's almost walked away from someone because she thought that she was being too emotional. Janelle didn't consider that she was a naturally emotional person and that she cried because that is her nature, not necessarily because of the relationship. Put it this way: If she measured friendships by tears, she would have broken ties with us, too.

Why are we women so emotional? Does it go back to childhood? Were we taught or expected to burst out crying when things didn't go our way? Janelle isn't the only woman who cries over everything. She is one of many who bases relationship decisions on what her heart feels at the moment or by the dreams she has at night. Research shows that the estrogen we produce in our bodies creates a stronger emotional flare for us than for men.

When you add that to the years of baby dolls, Easy-Bake ovens, and My Little Ponies, it's no wonder that we are more in touch with our emotional side than men are.

Some researchers believe that people behave as they do according to their "animal instincts." That is, nature has wired males one way, and females, another. According to this theory, we cannot help the way we are, and females are generally going to respond in a more emotional manner than males. Other researchers believe that people think and behave in certain ways because they are taught to do so, directly or indirectly. For example, a little girl may observe her mother and other female relatives weeping at the slightest upset. Or she may have learned at school among other children that girls are expected to display more emotion. The theory of women being more emotional than men thus becomes self-fulfilling, consciously or otherwise. I believe our feelings may be the result of a mixture of both concepts. Either way, we need to keep our emotions in perspective and rule them, rather than let them rule us!

Let's go back to Janelle. I mentioned that her personality was a little softer than my other girlfriends'. She is the type who rarely opens up unless it is something very pressing or extremely meaningful to her, and even then she can be somewhat constrained or reserved. With this, it's always a surprise when she wants to discuss her relationship, but I'm always here to listen.

Janelle came to me and said that she thought it was time to let go of the guy she had been dating after her breakup with Terrance. She was about to make the decision to cut her losses with him. Of course I knew why, but wanted to hear her say it,

"I think I am becoming too emotional over him, and it is too early in our relationship to be this emotional."

She didn't feel as if she should really be crying as much as she had been lately over things he had said or not said, or the activities they did or didn't do. I asked her why she was feeling so emotional, but she really didn't know, so she blamed it on the man in her life at the time. While it's true that a personal relationship often is the cause of stress or intense emotions that can shift rather suddenly from positive to negative, it seemed to me that Janelle really didn't have a clear perception of her relationship and that she ought to give herself time to figure out where the two of them were headed before taking the drastic step of breaking off their relationship. But all she kept saying was, "I shouldn't be in any relationship that brings me to tears."

She almost brought me to tears of exasperation!

Janelle felt her only solution was to break up with Dante, a man with many fine qualities that meshed well with Janelle's personality in general. She felt that he was her problem and the reason that she had been far too weepy lately, even though she couldn't clearly point to a particular reason or cause stemming from their relationship.

Let's rephrase. Because Janelle was shedding many tears with frequent thoughts of Dante, she thought that meant that she should break up with him. Janelle was turning the tables on herself! The fact is that Janelle's tears were only symptoms of her real problem. Simply put, Janelle is an overly emotional person. She can cry at the sight of a butterfly or the sound of a baby's cry. This was her problem, and she needed to solve it before running away from the relationship, too.

The issue was not Dante; it was just that Janelle was a crybaby. Seriously, this girl would cry over commercials if she watched them long enough. I reminded her that sensitivity is a gift that many women pray to have. She is just naturally inclined to be better in touch with her emotions than the average woman.

At this, Janelle laughed.

I asked her if she had *ever* asked Dante how he felt about her. She replied, "No."

I pointed out that she was about to make a major decision about their lives without finding out conclusively the answer to her question. I told her this would not be fair to Dante. I had to remind her that at the end of the day, it is possible that this man showed her in other ways how he cares for her. Just because he doesn't say or do or act in a manner to which she is accustomed, does this mean that he cares for her any less? If his actions are screaming that he is a good man, she would be crazy to push him away for something that many men are not easily capable of doing—expressing how they feel.

Now, let's take our "emotional versus rational" concept to the next level by continuing our exploration of Janelle's situation. Janelle decided to continue to date Dante. In the beginning, they talked on the phone for hours. They made plans to see each other each day and they spent a lot of time together. They were inseparable for a few weeks, but Janelle made it pretty clear that unless they were in a formal relationship that both considered as exclusive, she would continue to date others. Dante agreed and continued to date others as well.

As time went on, Dante continued to spend some time with Janelle, but she found herself inquiring more and more about what he was doing when he was not with her. These inquiries began after he said he would need to call her back, and failed to do so. The more he did this, the more she questioned his motives. The cycle progressed until finally Dante began disappearing for longer and longer periods of time. He wouldn't return her routine telephone calls or come over to visit when he promised he would. The interesting thing was that for some reason, Janelle noticed that she really began to care about his whereabouts and their relationship. She was hurt by his withdrawal and flagging commitment. She became confused and didn't know what to do. So, guess what she did? She became emotional, sobbing and crying her eyes out to each girlfriend who would spend time listening, patting her shoulder, and encouraging her to give up on Dante or give him more time to get back on track. In response, Janelle would cry harder and say she was confused; consequently, she took no action and the relationship grew stagnant.

Why is it that women are rational when it comes to decisions about staying in a class or dropping out, leaving a bad job or remaining, choosing the best meal for our kids at night or opting for a healthy restaurant alternative, but *all of a sudden* when we are dating, rationality goes out the door and we begin responding emotionally to every perceived incident of neglect or disrespect? Why do women get attached to men who could care less? When the inevitable happens and he fails to live up to our misplaced expectations, we respond based on how we feel instead of using our reasoning to address specific issues. Here is a truth for you: The moment we allow our emotions to be our guiding light, we become blind. You can't think clearly if you are confused, crying, frustrated, or depressed much of the time. It's okay to "cry it out" when you go off on an emotional jag for whatever reason—hormones, bickering, or anything, really. (It doesn't take much sometimes, right?) Just set the timer and give yourself a good five or ten minutes to weep, whine, or complain, and then—listen carefully now—get over it! Don't hang on to that heartache! Look for the sunshine in each day and cling to it. You will be surprised to find how easily your troubles can fade into the shadows when you chase after the brightness of each day's small joys.

When you are having problems with your guy, always make a conscious effort to listen to what he is really saying, and watch his actions closely. If Janelle had paid more attention to Dante's behavior in the very beginning, she would not be feeling so confused today. Dante started screaming that he had higher priorities than Janelle the first time he called her back a day after missing her call the night before.

Passion versus reason

Relationships should be all about passion, right? Why bother to get close to someone unless you can feel totally in love and abandon all caution? If you have to take time to think about where the relationship is headed or what you need to do to steer it in the right direction, that's too much work, isn't it? Love has everything to do with feelings and nothing to do with thought, wouldn't you agree?

Hold on a minute. When you go to the grocery store, do you ever take a shopping list? You don't want to forget the things you need or buy unnecessary (and potentially expensive) items, correct? Even though the enjoyment of food can involve creativity, spontaneity, and passion at times, often it centers on

Health Kick Sidebar:

Think of light and darkness. Darkness does not stem from any scientific formula. It is purely the absence of light. Cold is not significant to any scientific phenomenon. It is just the absence of heat. There is nothing mysterious about darkness and cold; each is just a consequence to light or heat being unavailable at certain times. In a parallel fashion, we women make choices more difficult than necessary. Could it be that the answer to your relationship dilemma is almost as easy as noticing the differences in light and dark, or heat and cold? Are we somehow making understanding these differences much harder than it needs to be? Probably so.

carefully choosing the right ingredients at the best price. Otherwise, the recipe might not turn out as planned. The same holds true for relationships. You may be able to generate passion with someone of low character or few morals, but how long will it last? How much will it cost emotionally? Passion has its place in romance, for sure, but so does reason. Don't go shopping for a man without taking your ingredient list, and don't settle for anything less than what you truly need to be happy.

"No man is perfect until you fall in love with him," is a quote by an unknown author. These words have great sincerity, in my opinion. I interpret this to mean that our blinders come on once we become attached to a person. We begin to overlook flaws and put aside everything that we have known to be true for this person, all because we are "in love." Once you fall for a person, you can become overly passionate in the fight to make things work between the two of you. It can also be very hard to read a man's ingredient label. It's kind of like being in the mood for hot chocolate while shopping at the grocery store. You purchase the first container of milk you find without checking the expiration date. You are in so great a hurry to eat your favorite food that you rip off the top without adequate precautions, only to find it is unfit to drink. No matter how passionate you are for a relationship, make yourself slow down and read that man's ingredients before you do anything!

Like some of us women, Janelle's passion for her relationship caused her to identify most, if not all, aspects of her life with her relationship to Dante (or to Terrance, the salesman, when she was with him). If she was happy, it was because of him. If she felt depressed, it was Dante's fault. If she succeeded, it was due in part to his love and support. If she fell short or failed, it was because she was too preoccupied with him and their relationship. This is not a healthy way to manage a personal relationship! Ladies, we must take responsibility for our own happiness, actions, and decisions. We have to acknowledge, at least to a certain degree, the separateness of our individuality and identity from the man in our lives. Although we can forge an emotional chain of connection, that chain should never become a lifeline, not even after marriage. Yes, in marriage, two become united as a single legal entity. But even then, women often maintain their own jobs, bank accounts, and even a few female friends that are not necessarily part of their "couples" entertainment. The emotional connection that holds two people together should provide a means of communication and expressing affection, or of combining strength and wisdom to solve problems. But it should not be viewed by either member of the relationship as the ultimate source of all joy, fulfillment, hardship, or failure. We must become responsible for our own success or failure, and not be so ready to blame the man we love for the passionate highs and lows in life.

If you find yourself becoming a little too passionately dependent on the man you are seeing, ask yourself why this is happening. Is it because of his demands, or your insecurity? If you are thinking about him too much or worrying about him too often, you may need to take a deep breath and step back from the relationship to analyze it before you break it off. A timeout can come in handy for this purpose. Of course, if there are issues of abuse, infidelity, or illicit activity, you need to take immediate action to separate yourself from these problems and the man involved with them. But if you are unsure of the reason for your anxieties, spend some time discussing your concerns with that special guy to see if, together, you can figure out what's going on. Alternatively, you may find it helpful to meet with a relationship therapist for objective feedback about your feelings.

My friends are making me so confused when I am the only one who knew [him] truly. My girlfriends are beginning to sound like voices in my head. I don't know what to do. All I want to do sometimes is cry like a newborn baby. To love someone and give them everything you have tends to hurt when it is not returned. It hurts like hell.

~age nineteen

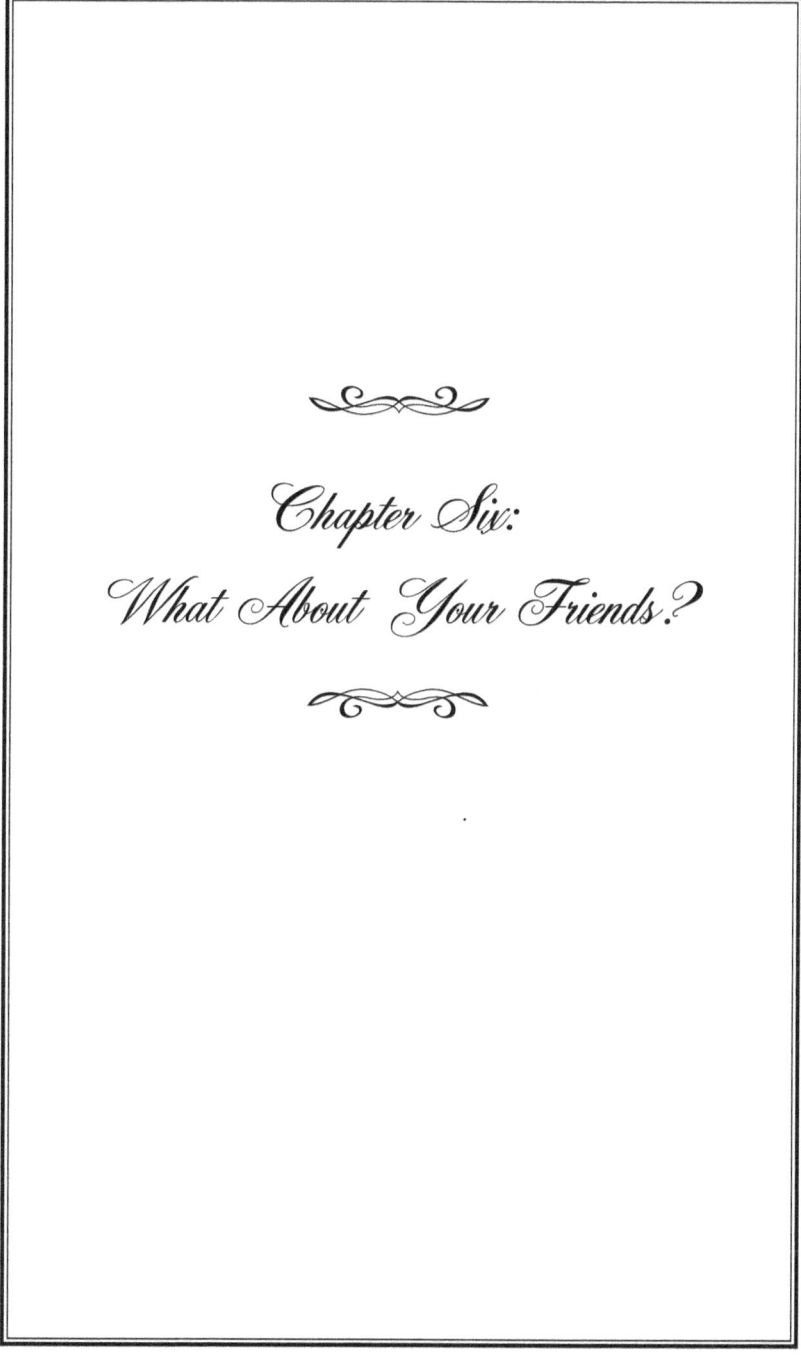

Chapter Six:

What About Your Friends?

Going shopping with friends can be fun! They can give you new ideas for recipes, or recommend new foods and products that you should try. Their creative ideas and helpful suggestions can make even the most boring shopping trip less tedious. On the other hand, sometimes we also know that it can become a little too much. Let me explain.

When I was an undergraduate student at Virginia Tech, I used to braid hair out of my small eight hundred-square-foot, two-bedroom apartment shared with my sister. I had many repeat customers, from other undergraduates to masters or doctoral students, to neighbors who lived and worked in nearby communities. You can imagine how many men and women I used to meet on a regular basis. My hobby was great for networking, but what I appreciated more were the talks I had with the female clients. Women always discussed men and relationships, and encouraging advice often was given and received.

Of all of the advice I received, Tina's stood out the most. I believe I was about eighteen years old, and she was around twenty-six, and knowledgeable as well as sharp, witty, and pretty popular, so of course I was going to listen. She told me to watch what I told my girlfriends about my relationships. When you have problems with a man, it is important to be careful not to share too much with your friends, especially if you know you will probably remain in a relationship with the man you were just crying about. She said that it is difficult for those who love you to be as forgiving of your guy as you have been. Should you decide to take him back, they may not bring him back into their lives. Although the notion of your girlfriends not forgiving or accepting your boyfriend may seem silly, it can become a lot more serious. If your relationship is in distress, the tension of your girlfriends hating your guy and your guy disrespecting your girlfriends only causes more confusion and stress. And it's no one's fault but your own.

You probably don't seek much advice when planning your grocery shopping list, so why would you ask for suggestions when shopping for a guy? When it comes to taking advice from girlfriends, remember three things. One, they are only human. Most of the advice they give you will be based on biases from their past experiences and environments. Two, no one truly understands the entire situation that you and your partner are experiencing. It is difficult to make a good decision with partial facts, especially facts based on only one person's side of the story. Three, your girlfriends have their own motives. Now, these motives may be good and sincere, or they can be bad and disruptive. The good motives are the ones by which your girlfriends are trying to protect you and make you happy. The bad motives come from the girlfriends who don't want to be the only single girl left. They encourage you to let your man go under any circumstance, because that means they can finally have their bar-hopping buddy back. For this type of girlfriend, it is very difficult when everyone around her is in a seemingly great relationship. All her friends are happy, but not her. Although they support your relationship, they have no problem pulling you away if you allow them to. They will do everything they can to make sure that you know that all men are dogs, and that you will never be able to find a good one, just like them. In other words, if you don't find the perfect cut of steak at the supermarket, give up and go vegetarian—*like they did.*

As a side note, be very wary of the Quadrant Four girlfriend— the Enhanced Water. She is the one who will easily slide right into your spot should you decide to let your boyfriend go. She is waiting for you to let him go, and she is the biggest cheerleader for you during your release process. This girl is ready and willing to take him off of your hands if either you or your man gives her the opportunity to do so. This happened to me once in college while I was dating a guy who hailed from Quadrant Two, the Cigarette. Now, we will call this Enhanced Water girl Brandy. Brandy was a sophomore when I was a junior. She was one of my hair-braiding clients. We talked a lot about random things and quickly learned we had some things in common. I have to admit that I didn't know a lot about her, and that was one of my biggest mistakes. Do not tell all of your business to a girl that you barely know! But I was young, and so she and I became closer. At the time I was going through some things with the Cigarette guy. The more emotional I became over him, the more she was available for me to talk to. I mean, she would come by my job, come to my dorm room, call me on the phone, and walk with me to meetings in order to be the shoulder that I needed to cry on. I wasn't in my right mind, and I continuously poured out my feelings to her about the guy I was dating and how things weren't working out between us anymore.

I finally found out that she and he were messing around behind my back. It had been going on for a few weeks before I knew about it. My Cigarette boyfriend was the one who confessed. She would have never told me—and that's the sad part. No need to feel sorry for me because of that situation—just use my lesson as a foundation in the deciding to allow someone in your circle that you barely know. Fool me once, huh?

Another lesson to learn is that you don't have to tell your girlfriends every time you slip and eat a Snickers bar! This means that you will probably date a guy or two that you aren't the most proud of—*perhaps while on rebound*. So, unless you are certain that your healthy eating kick is over, you may want to keep this to yourself. Here are a few reasons.

Understand that you are these friends' first and only priority. They know that Jimmy this month, was Jerald two months ago, and will be James next week. Why would they care more for him than you? The person you are dating is not a priority to them. As your friend, a woman who really cares about you understands that her job is not to keep you two together; it is to protect you. She is only trying to do what she believes is her job. What kind of friend would she be to encourage healing and restoration of a failing relationship?

Confusion can result when you share your personal business with women who may have a personal axe to grind. Talking to your girlfriends can create panic in your life that wouldn't have been there otherwise. They might advise you to get revenge or to make a fool of yourself to spite him. I used to have a girlfriend in college who was always ready and willing to slit tires, if needed. I think everyone has had this type of girlfriend. They mean well, but their advice can fall a little short of where you need it to be. You should find one person who you can trust and whose opinion you value. This will be a girlfriend who understands that there is a time to listen and a time to give advice. You should talk to someone who truly cares about what makes you happy as well as what is good for you, and who is able to be candid in a way that allows you to make your own decisions. As a rule of thumb, when something is bothering me in a relationship and I need outside advice, I love talking to securely married women. I find they give the most logical suggestions because chances are they have been in my position and somehow came through it successfully. They have nothing to gain from my success or failure; they will be cheering for my well-being and happiness. But that's just my opinion!

The final verdict on how to respond to a problem in your relationship is always your decision! No one is better suited than you and your man to know all of the ins and outs of everything that you have experienced as a couple. For others to tell you that you should stay with him—*no matter what*—or move on is unheard of. That's just like someone telling you that you are crazy for sneaking that Snickers bar without understanding that you had planned to eat it in order to treat yourself. How can they make a decision for you with only a quarter of the facts available? The decision is yours, so be careful with it.

Health Kick Sidebar:

Advice is the most valuable gift a trusted person may provide. Notice how I've listened to many people along the way who have all given me advice that I use today. But take all of the advice you get with a grain of salt. You do not need to go through every situation in order to be wise. You can observe other people's situations and learn from them. Carefully sift through advice given by understanding the motives of the person giving it to you. Bank this valuable advice and use or pass it on when necessary. Understand when it is important to give advice to another, and keep your motives in check. One of my close friends keeps a journal. She writes everything in this special tool. She writes down the pieces of advice that she needs and when the time is right, she can regurgitate this counsel and use it in a positive manner.

I had something good, but I feel like I've tainted it like I seem to do with every relationship. I push and push and push for better until I accidentally push them away.

~age twenty-one

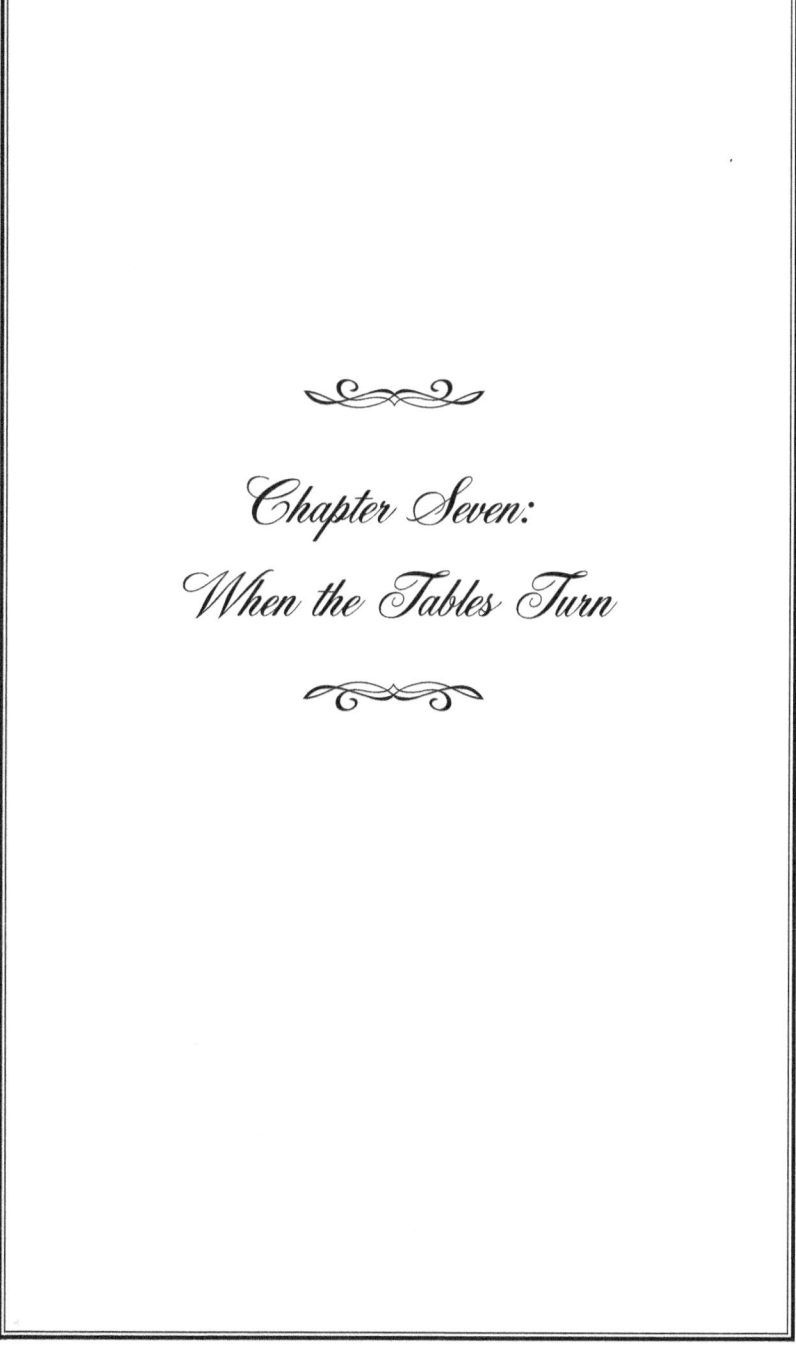

Chapter Seven:
When the Tables Turn

Some women will buy anything on sale. They can't resist a discount or the lure of double coupon day. Even if it's a product they don't like or probably won't use, they are unable to get past that attractive display at the end of Aisle Four. It's on display for a reason, right? It was meant to be purchased!

Sheila is like that. She is attracted to a man only if others also find him alluring—if he is on display, so to say. The reason for the attraction isn't as important, but if he is in the limelight, she would like to be there with him.

I remember back in the day, one guy in particular chased Sheila for years. His name was Daniel. Daniel was lovesick over her and would have given his right arm to date her. The issue was that he wasn't very popular. He didn't get a lot of attention, but his friends did. The group that he hung out with was pretty popular; they were all football and basketball players. Sheila had chased one guy in the clique, Justin, for years, even though he never showed much interest in her. After a few years of this, Daniel finally moved on and started dating a nice woman who was also interested in him. He went on to enlist in the air force. He kept the same girlfriend, and their relationship was strong and solid.

When he returned from duty, this man had changed in many ways. The little Danny that we had known before had become rugged, strong Daniel. People instantly noticed the change. He had exchanged his eyeglasses for contact lenses, and his shyness had evolved into confidence. As other women began to notice these interesting changes, so did Sheila. Ironically, she finally accepted the fact that she and Justin would never become a twosome, and she began focusing her attention on Daniel, who was acclimating to civilian life.

Sheila wanted Daniel for herself. She became obsessed with him, just as she had been with the high-school star Justin, and she spent the next three years chasing him to try to get Daniel back. But Daniel didn't want anything to do with Sheila. He remembered how she had dismissed him earlier while in hot pursuit of the "cool guy," Justin.

This happens so often! I can't count the number of times I've seen a woman let a healthy Vegetable or a luscious Hot Pepper escape her grocery cart and then regret it later. Remember, he may not come in the best package, but the ingredients he is made of could be exactly what you need in your life. When you shop for fresh fruit or vegetables, the peel is only part of the picture. Even bananas with bruises or cucumbers with soft spots can be valuable in a special recipe.

Let's discuss another example of how the tables can turn. Do you remember the guy I dated in college who would always start random, introspective conversations? Well, one day he told me something that hurt my feelings and threw me for a loop. He said that all that had happened in our relationship (the cheating, lies, deception, loneliness, and frustration) was no longer his fault; he claimed it was mine because I had allowed it to happen.

Ha! Can you believe it? He told me that our relationship problems were my entire fault!

I couldn't speak for a few seconds. So, clearly, he had time to elaborate. This man said that every time I left him for disrespecting me, cheating on me, or neglecting me, and then came running back to him it was my decision. It wasn't his choice. It wasn't him that hurt my feelings or made me cry. My pain was the result of my decision to come back!

In other words, the day I became aware of my guy's ingredient label and yet still continued to date him, I became the responsible party since I had knowingly returned to a situation that was less than satisfactory. Still, I continued to give him my most valuable asset: my time. Anything that happened from then on, I seemed to be giving him tacit permission to do. I never gave him a reason to question his actions. Why should he? I accepted his problem behavior and took him back, no matter what situations had fed my distrust and despair. Fool me once, shame on you. Fool me twice, shame on me. Isn't that how the saying goes?

The same goes for you. If you are with a man who is making you miserable, and you have come to the realization that his behavior is not likely to change, the choice of response is up to you. If you decide to stick it out, you have no one to blame but yourself. Whatever he does from here on out is no longer his fault because you have made the choice to stay with him and accept his mistreatment. Through your actions, you are telling your guy that you will tolerate his disrespect and dishonesty. You have become an accessory after the fact—his accomplice, if you will.

Tracy had been calling her boyfriend, Sonny, all weekend. She was worried that something bad might have happened. It was unlike him not to answer her telephone call, at least in the two months they had been dating. Finally, by Sunday, he answered his phone. Breathlessly, Tracy explained that she had been very worried about Sonny, and all she wanted to know was if everything was okay. Sonny paused, but then admitted that he had been upset by a comment Tracy had made on Friday, so he had needed some time to think before giving her a call back.

Okay, I know you are taking a deep breath right now. That's what I did, too.

As I listened to Tracy's story, I couldn't help but ask her what comment he was referring to. She said, "I told him that I needed more of his time, because lately he hadn't been spending any with me." *This is what made him upset!* Now, I always remind my girls that it is human nature to "push the envelope." What you must remember is that the moment you start tolerating some small, inappropriate attitude, language, or behavior, human nature is to push for something a little larger the next time. Tracy had a decision to make.

Ladies, stop participating in your own relational abuse! Don't be a silent witness or a slave to your man's misguided morals. It's one thing for a man to take advantage of you until you find out and put a stop to it. But it's another when you learn the truth and continue enabling him to misuse you. Read those ingredient descriptions carefully, girlfriends! Find out what that desirable-looking package actually contains inside. That delectable-looking gourmet meal may turn

Health Kick Sidebar:

Sometimes you can look at your situation and learn that no one else is hurting you. You are the reason why you are unhappy! Certain circumstances are caused only by you. Sometimes you have to learn how to move out of your own way! You are the only shadow between your current situation and the future you have always hoped for. Allow yourself to be happy—the first time.

out to be ruined when you remove the wrapping. Then, if you choose to eat spoiled and unwholesome food, you have to take responsibility for your choices and not blame anyone else, including the guy who is preying on your good nature.

This is kind of hard for me. [He] called me tonight. I honestly thought that I would never hear from him again. It hurt me to have to tell him that I don't miss him or think about him anymore. I told him that I didn't want to see him again, and I finally made him believe that I meant it. I had begged him not to wait until it was too late ... but he did. Now I'm gone and I have no plans to come back. He wouldn't be with me because of our past—that's funny—because now he's a part of it!

~age twenty-one

Chapter Eight:
Women Decide

Sometimes you buy a bag of potatoes at the store and open it at home to find the entire bunch is spoiled. You have a couple of choices at that point: You can either peel them as best you can to salvage the sections that can be eaten, or you can return the bag to the store for a refund. Only someone who isn't thinking straight would cook the potatoes without removing the bad parts and hoping they won't get sick. Most of us would avoid the rotten produce altogether. Either way—you decide!

A girlfriend of mine, Rebecca, made a profound statement one day.

"Most women are in love with their man. We love who he is inside as well as the packaging outside. We work at understanding his character and appreciating his personality."

Rebecca went on to add that it doesn't matter where each relationship partner is in life, because if the situation changes for almost any reason, or if his or her circumstances are altered, a woman typically will remain devoted to her man because he hasn't changed.

Conversely, Rebecca explained that she feels most men fall in love with the relational situation: how comfortable he feels around his woman, what she looks like (at home and in public), how independent she is, their life together, and their social connectivity with others. But if any aspect of their romantic or relational situation changes, he begins to believe that he is not in love anymore; for many men, the situation becomes potentially confusing or unstable. Then, he leaves. Even if he doesn't abandon his lady physically, many men leave mentally and emotionally.

Isn't that a fascinating concept? It really resonated with me.

Let me introduce you to Rebecca.

Rebecca was a dreamer. She was the kind of girl who wanted the storybook relationship and believed that she deserved it. She loved to love, but she couldn't find a person who wanted to return her level of affection in a way that she could recognize. Rebecca would blindly throw herself into the social realm by being honest about her feelings, expressing her desire for a husband and children, and telling a man everything that she needed early in a relationship. Overall, Rebecca was blatantly honest because that was the only way she knew to be genuine in a relationship.

Then Rebecca started dating Tim. Now, Tim was tall with a light complexion; he had the kind of look that most women find very attractive. Some might say he was overly handsome. Tim was nice to Rebecca, but just not that honest with her about his true feelings regarding what he wanted the relationship to be. Tim wanted a simpler level of commitment, but Rebecca didn't notice Tim's reticence, because from her perspective, what a man says means more than how he acts. She believed that a man can be trusted to live by his word, and Tim said all the right things.

So Rebecca continued dating Tim. Yes, she knew that her relationship was unhealthy because, although Tim said that he wanted to marry her, have children, and live the family lifestyle, his actions suggest he didn't want a permanent commitment. He spent much of his free time with his friend and he avoided Rebecca's calls. All this showed he wasn't as interested in the storybook life as Rebecca longed to believe. She understood that Tim was clearly in the shaded zone of the matrix because he could never be found; he told her that he was feeling too much pressure and he thought they were moving too fast. He stopped spending quality time with Rebecca. Although Tim continued to be nice to her when they were together, his emotions had already strayed. When he left Rebecca's presence, she was out of his mind, although she continued to think about Tim with great affection.

Rebecca witnessed all the signs that this relationship needed to end, but she could not decide what to do. So she did absolutely nothing except wait, wait, and wait some more. Sitting around, night after night, Rebecca kept hoping each phone call and text message was from Tim, but his communication gradually decreased and all but disappeared. She wanted to believe that if she waited long enough, Tim would come around to her point of view and align his actions with his promises. Eventually he would keep his word, right? Rebecca trusted that while she waited for Tim at home each evening, seldom going out except for an occasional dinner with a concerned girlfriend, Tim was going to miraculously awaken from his lack of appreciation for who she was and how good they could be together, and someday he would change.

But in the midst of doing nothing, Rebecca was teaching Tim how to treat her, revealing her ever-declining standards and her vulnerability to his empty promises. As she accepted the dwindling attention and shrinking quality time that he gave her, Tim continued to make the most of his bargain by giving Rebecca as little as he could get away with. Why not? She was willing to tolerate his disinterest and limited availability. In effect, Rebecca was figuratively screaming to him, "Keep treating me the way you do. I am not going anywhere. Watch me—*you can depend on it*—I'll be here for you."

She and I shared this conversation one day at my kitchen table:

Rebecca said, "I want to wait it out. I want to be available until the very end because I have to know for myself that I have done all I can do to keep this relationship together." The look of tension on her face belied her self-convincing words.

"Has he called you lately at all?" I asked.

"No," she sighed, struggling not to break down in tears.

"What was the last thing he said to you?" I asked gently, offering to pour more wine.

She sniffed. "He said, 'I don't have time for this' and walked out on me," she said.

"Hmm. So what do you think you should do?" I asked.

"Wait ..." she sobbed. "I don't know what to do without him."

Wouldn't most of us agree that Rebecca's response to Tim's behavior is somewhat self-defeating? But her mind was made up, and nothing I said seemed to make a difference.

Every day, men make decisions about the women in their lives—rational decisions. Let me give you an example. Because many men naturally have a conquering nature, they typically nurture a goal relating to women. A male friend told me that a man's goal is to conquer a woman, whether by proving his masculinity in a sexual relationship or by becoming more invested in an emotional way. Another friend commented that most single men make the decision to pursue a relationship only after sex has taken place. A man wants to find out if he still feels the same about a woman after sex, or if it was just the "thrill of the chase" that kept him going after her. Regardless of whether people would agree or disagree with these statements, these are clear examples that men understand the power that they have in their own decision making. He will make a decision about whether to stay with the current romantic interest in his life or let her go so he can pursue a new female.

As terrible as those examples sound, at least most men feel in control of the situation because they have a game plan in mind. Why are we not thinking the same way? Whether it is two months or two years into the relationship, where does our control go?

Why is it such a draining process for women to make relationship decisions? We are taught, along with the boys, that decisions of the will involve "mind over matter." This means that we must learn to control our emotions in order to make rational choices. If this is the case, then why do we women feel as though our option to stay with or leave a man has been taken away from us the moment we fall in love, the moment we have sex, the moments when we go out on a few dates? I am sick and tired of hearing things like, "I love him too much to let him go," "I can't leave him," or, "I'm not strong enough to stay away from him." In my earlier life, I reached the point of frustration and futility in saying those things, too. We use excuses to say, "I don't have a choice." What we don't seem to realize is that when we do nothing, we are still making a decision that results in consequences.

> **Health Kick Sidebar:**
>
> *Relational decisions are the focal point of everything we do. We decide to be in relationships and then we choose to walk away from them. We decide to shop in one quadrant or we change our minds and shop in another. We entertain nonsense or we make the decision not to. This book is based on the decisions we make as women. We need to embrace the fact that most events in our lifetime are not just in direct response to the decisions we make, but also to those we believe we aren't making.*

Let me say this one more time. Is everyone listening?

Not making a decision is making a decision!

We women believe there must be a magical formula or a sign from above to help us choose the best path in a given relationship. What we don't realize is that the facts are already before us if we allow ourselves to look for them, analyze them, and respond to them in a conscientious and responsible manner.

Ask yourself this: Is he really what you are looking for? Is he as good to you as you deserve? Is he making you happy? If your answer is no, and you know that you don't want to be in a relationship without these things, you need to move on.

You can stand and stare at that bag of chips at the grocery store for several moments, knowing you shouldn't have them but very tempted to buy them anyway. If you read the ingredients, you will find some things to consider carefully, such as the amount of salt and fat (including trans-fat), along with the absence of meaningful nutrition. Are the chips worth the price of purchase and the guilt you will feel afterward? If so, go for it! At least you have weighed the pros and cons. But don't pick up some chips at the store, come home and eat them, and then wail that you're putting on extra pounds. Acknowledge your responsibility to know what you are putting into your body, as well as the probable after-effects, physical *and* emotional.

For once, I've made the right decision in my own life. Yesterday, I wrote a long-awaited letter telling him that I had to let him go. He and I have been on and off continuously for almost ten months, and things don't appear to be any healthier in our relationship. Oprah made a comment yesterday that confirmed all of my feelings. She said, "If you find yourself looking through your man's things or spying/following him to find out what he was doing, you are at an all-time low." I knew that I needed to make some changes. This is really going to hurt now, but later this will be better for me. God knows what's best, and he laid this feeling on my heart for a reason. I've been feeling out of character for a while, and I truly need to take this time to work on me.

~age twenty-two

Chapter Nine:

You Don't Always Have to Prove It

Have you ever had someone come over to you and say, "Smell this—it smells horrible!"

The person's facial expression even confirms that the smell coming from that moldy container left far too long in your refrigerator is pretty disgusting. To this day, I still don't understand why someone would walk over and smell the container in response. Why not just take the other person's word for it? I would! To me, if it looks moldy and my friend's facial expression and words confirm my thoughts, that's all I need. Point proven! I don't have to walk over and taste it to know that it smells horrible. So why are we guilty of this in relationships?

I believe there are two types of "prove-it-to-me" women. The first must see things through to the end to exhaust every conceivable option that might preserve or prolong the relationship.

The second type is the one who has to see things for herself. This woman must physically catch her guy committing an indiscretion before she can walk away from the relationship. Neither woman will leave until she is forced to, by which time she most likely has accumulated a significant amount of emotional baggage. Of course, it's possible that either type of female will have gone into a relationship of this nature with some emotional issues to begin with. But staying involved with an unwholesome man who's just plain not good for her is bound to add to her overall confusion about relationships, men, and her self-esteem.

It's one thing to have trust. Most of us want to see the good side of the people we care about. We're looking for a person's best qualities and often will take someone's word at face value, at least until facts prove otherwise. But it's another thing to allow your pride to keep you in an unhealthy situation even as facts emerge to contradict what the man in your life insists to be truth. Some women just don't want to admit to anyone—even themselves—

that they have made a mistake in judgment or have been made a fool of by someone for whom they have begun experiencing strong feelings and a relational commitment.

I remember it as if it were yesterday. Erin and I were enthusiastic teens doing well with grades and extracurricular activities in high school when she said to me,

"Before I ever leave Lance, I have to see it [his infidelity] for myself."

She was saying that before she would give up on her relationship, she needed to see unequivocal proof that Lance was not being faithful. In other words, no matter how many rumors or confirmed sightings of his infidelity Erin might receive from trusted friends or other witnesses, she would reject them all until she caught him in "the act." Today, Erin is almost thirty years old, married to Lance, and has two of his children. Over the years, many of our high school friends have witnessed Lance cheating on Erin in some capacity or another, from having dinner with another woman in a restaurant to talking intimately with a female in his car. Lance even confessed to me that he had walked into the marriage planning to keep his relationships on the side. All the while, he kept his alternative lifestyle hidden from his wife. Although I am sure that every ounce in her knows that he is unfaithful, ten years later she is still waiting to see it for herself. Erin probably knows full well this is highly unlikely to happen unless her guy wants to be caught, so their "secret" is safe, and she can rest easy, knowing she will never be put to the final test and have to give up her husband. So she can smoke her Cigarette guy, feeling totally at ease at least with her friends, although privately she must endure a terrible agony, wondering if she will catch him in bed with another woman someday.

But I don't know why I am talking about Erin, because I was just like her. I had to learn my lesson the hard way. I was in a relationship with a guy who was even worse than the Cigarette guy in Quadrant Two. He fell into the "toxic substances" category, if there were such a thing. Being with this guy was like destroying my body with cocaine, but I wasn't able to see this until after the fact. This guy was good at convincing me that I was the only woman in his life. He could even make me feel guilty for suspecting him. Many times I reached low points within the relationship because I had to prove that he was cheating on me so I could have the strength to get up and walk away from him. Time after time I found strong evidence that should have convinced me to take a stand and leave the guy, but I stayed. This man could carry a lie until the very end, and I was committed enough to accept pretty much whatever he chose to tell me. Good love overlooks a fault or mistake, but this kind of oversight goes beyond "good" to "enabling," which didn't help either him or me.

One time, a woman walked up to me at a club and gloated that she was dating my guy. She said to me, "How in the world are you with him, if he is always at my house?" She said this in the most serious and most gut-wrenching tone.

I can laugh now because it is funny, but believe me, it wasn't funny then. My response was, "I travel all the time."

And that was the truth, but I can't believe that this was my response to her. In reality, I was always out of town for work. The three of us were in this club at the same time, and he still wiggled his way out of it, saying that she was lying, that there was nothing going on between the two of them, that she was a lesbian and was being vengeful because someone he knew had mistreated her. What's interesting is that I didn't believe him, but because I didn't have the proof, I let it go and stayed with him. It was easier not to rock the boat, even though he had emotionally rocked my world. At that point in time, I was no better than Erin.

Even detectives and lawyers don't win every case with only tangible evidence. Sometimes they have to allow their God-given instincts to lead the way. I should have known better. Erin should know better now. There were times when I even began looking for evidence around this guy's apartment. By now you know how sticky a situation can become if you start searching for evidence against your man. As the adage goes, if you look hard enough, you will find something. Yet I don't recommend this approach because it will just drive you crazy.

Being the woman who has to see things through until the end or the woman who has to see things for her own self can only prolong the inevitable. We are afraid of what we may have to do with the truth. Do we now have to do what we've promised and leave? Do we have to now face others to say, "You were right?" It's hard to face those who wag their fingers in your face, saying "I told you so." And it's hard to accept that all the time and energy you've invested in this relationship has gone to waste. Plus, no one likes to admit they've been taken advantage of.

I have met many women who must see things through until the end—hoping the end will never come. So much time has been invested that they feel they can't walk away: not now, not ever. It could be because of the children, the fear of being alone, or the worry that no one is better than the man they are leaving. Maybe they want to prove their friends wrong when they predict the relationship won't last. Whatever the case, you will not be the one to break up. It has to be him, whether by getting caught, leaving you first, or ending up in jail or dead. You find yourself yelling at him every day to just tell you the truth: If he doesn't want to be with you anymore, he should just say so. But he won't.

You are crying every night because you know that it's over, but the only proof that the relationship has ended is when you push him to his limit with your tears and screaming and he finally yells, "I'm done!"

And then you have the nerve to be shocked over something you already knew and blamed him for over many months or years of hurt and deceit, when in fact you allowed it—and even encouraged it—to continue. Get over yourself, girl, and realize that this man did you no favors. You deserve better! You should go out there and get it. At the end of the day, if it looks like a frog, smells like a frog, and hops like a frog— then why do you keep kissing it, hoping for a prince? Girl, it's a frog.

Health Kick Sidebar:

Although I do believe there is a purpose behind every situation we experience, I don't believe that it will always be clearly understood. You may only go through your situation so you can turn around and help the next person through a similar situation. Only God knows why I've had to go through so much drama with men and dating, but if I hadn't, I wouldn't have had anything to share with you.

I met a girl in church once who really helped me to get through a breakup and the only favor that she asked was that I return the favor to the next girl who will go through the same thing. I hope that you decide to do the same.

Sometimes when something hurts, you think it is going to last forever. You believe that you will never get over it. Then one day you do. All you seem to remember is how you've prayed to God the night before to make everything okay. And one day—He does. We get over hurts by the grace of God. I am over him only by the grace of God. I haven't seen him in six months.

~age twenty-one

Chapter Ten:

When it's Time to Let Go

Every woman has her relationship breaking point. It is the point of no return.

I could sense that Toni was reaching hers when she finally asked me for some real advice. In the beginning, Toni was in denial and didn't want to hear any negative comments about Doug or their relationship, but I could tell this time was different. Serious and sad, Toni said that no matter how well she understood that Doug wasn't the best for her, she felt like she should still hold on to him and help him become a better man. He would not be able to do better without her.

"He needs me," she said with a trace of desperation that left no doubt about who really needed whom.

I told her that we women have been able to hold the world on our shoulders by caring for aging parents, young children, a home, and a career and still set our personal goals and accomplish them. If Toni really wanted to hold on to this man, she could do so, but she ought to make herself a promise first: Hold on to him only until she could feel herself falling backward. At that time she should commit to letting him go. No questions asked. That would be the kindest promise she could keep to herself.

If you are in Toni's situation and decide to stay in the relationship to go that extra mile for your guy, you have to realize that you may be doing it alone, without his equal level of commitment, and perhaps very little support from friends and family. What if you reach the point of falling backwards? What if, by that time, your relationship is draining all of your energy and emotional reserves? You have recognized that you are standing in the shaded zone, and that the very product you have chosen as a relational nutrient is one of the worst things for you. You know that you are unhappy, but you also know that you are in love. You have a second decision to make. A choice is before you.

You no longer have the option of being in love and being happy. Only healthy relationships offer that option. Now is that time to consider which is more important to you. Would you rather be in love or be happy? *Let me repeat that for you fast readers out there:*

Would you rather be in love or be happy?

Somewhere along the path of love, happiness has veered off and you are at a fork in the road. Which way will you travel? One will be sacrificed for the other. Are you prepared? Can you endure?

Choosing love is easy at first, but the consequences of this choice become more difficult with time. With this option, you will choose to stay in your relationship for immediate convenience and temporary joy. A benefit of this option is that you will be able to stay by his side and keep your life steady for the moment. He is still a part of it, and at the moment you are content. You can indefinitely put off the pain of a breakup and the mourning period that will follow.

The disadvantage is that you will remain alongside the man who is draining you in many critical ways, and it is almost certain that your situation will not change. For now you are burying inevitable feelings of loneliness, sadness, pain, and loss in order to have the comfort of knowing that he is still a part of your life, but these feelings will eventually be exhumed by his doing the same things he has been doing—and the cycle will continue until you break it.

Remember Janelle and Dante? Janelle started to have feelings for Dante, until he frequently disappeared on her and started missing her phone calls, not calling back as promised. Well, not long after that Janelle told me that she was no longer planning to pursue him. But when Dante caught wind of her decision, he became focused on their relationship again, and after a few phone calls and some major convincing, Janelle was back in the relationship. Dante acted fine for a week or so, but then went right back to his old missing-in-action ways. Janelle should have held out for some type of proof that Dante was serious about investing in their relationship, but she caved in and was put through the cycle yet again.

Choosing happiness is the other option. Who would have ever imagined that choosing happiness would be so difficult? The truth is, it will be difficult at first, but the joy of independence and self-reliance becomes easier as time goes on. With this option you will have to make a decision to walk away from your unhealthy relationship, like giving up smoking or fattening desserts. This will be a decision that will crush you in the beginning. I call this the "walking up out of it" phase.

"Walking up out of it" is a decision that says you must get "through" it; you can't get "around" it. When you walk up out of it, you don't know where you are going or how you are going to get there, or if anything will be waiting for you when you arrive. All you do know is that the current situation is not where you are supposed to be. This is not where you want to be, and you know you deserve better. True, you will feel loneliness, sadness, pain, hurt, and perhaps even abandonment, but eventually these difficult emotions will be replaced with a sense of understanding, and then a sense of self-made happiness. Just know that you are going to go through withdrawal right now, but that it will get better. People escape addictions all the time, and you can, too. Being a healthy consumer takes effort, but learning to select the best nutrients for your body and mind will restore a sense of ownership to your life and lead to healthy results in a short time, if you stick with it.

As for your former relationship, you still may have dozens of questions while you are walking up out of it. You may not understand what happened, why it happened the way it did, and what the future holds for the two of you. You may never know the whole truth, but because you are no longer blind or too emotional to be rational, you may begin to have a more balanced understanding of what took place. Understanding has always come to the patient and seeking ones.

Should he call you again—as most of them do—here is one piece of advice for you. Let the phone ring through the first time. Don't answer it! Why? You need some time to think through the what-ifs.

Health Kick Sidebar:

When we walk away from a man and/or a relationship, we must keep our sights set on the future. No relationship is a total loss. Afterward, as you work through the healing phase of recovery, take time to reflect on what happened, and why, and how you will do things differently in the future. If you are a "good" woman with several great qualities, you will still find yourself falling into the zone of "the girl who got away." This will probably happen more than once in your lifetime. Has a guy ever told you that you are the one who got away, and that in the back of his mind, he will always care about you? I can't tell you how many men have contacted me in some manner to say that I am the one who got away. The moral of the story is that it's okay. You can't be the special girl for every man; you are not going to be everyone's type, and you won't always be his first choice. Men (and women) can settle for women (and men) and do so every day. Sometimes a man does not want to become a better person, but he knows that you will not accept any less. It's okay if you let this type of man leave. Not every good man is meant to be with you and you are not available for all of those good guys out there.

If you are wondering whether or not to answer that phone, I want you to remember why you left him in the first place. Take a moment to travel back to that place and time when you were feeling miserable, lost, and forsaken. What was the reason for those terrible feelings? Now ask yourself, what are the odds of it happening again with this guy? How many times did it happen before? Do you want to take the chance of going through that pain all over again? If your answer is yes, then finally answer the phone or call him back. If your answer is no, let his call go to voice mail. And if you find that you are stronger than you ever imagined, try deleting his voice mail instead of listening to it and tell yourself, "He can't talk his way back in this time."

I always tell my girlfriends that when it comes to making a decision to leave a man, you shouldn't have any expectations about what the future holds for you and him. He may call again; he may not. He may care that you are gone; he may not. He may check on you to make sure that you are okay, or he may not. When you decide to leave, you are also responsible for leaving those expectations behind. At this point, the only person who matters is you. I've seen women try to make it easy for a man to find them, in case the man wants to apologize or ask for a second chance. This is what I call leaving breadcrumbs. Ladies, stop leaving those breadcrumbs behind. A great woman once told me that if a man wants you back badly enough, he will find you, even if you are under a rock. You do not have to make it easy for him. So do something more constructive with those breadcrumbs, like feeding them to the birds!

It's amazing how a breath of fresh air is exactly what it is supposed to be. The air at night has this fascinating way of calming a soul. Although cold and icy, it still seems to remain so abundant that I do not have to share it. A breath of fresh air almost makes you believe that all of the problems you once thought you had are now long gone and far out of the picture. A breath is something that "we" commonly take for granted, but it is so needed. My soul was uneasy tonight. I almost did not know how to respond.

~ age twenty-two

Chapter Eleven:
Trouble Leads to Blessings

One Saturday evening my friend Tracy came over to catch up on old times over a spaghetti and wine dinner. When I asked how her relationship with Sonny was going, she twirled some pasta around her fork, gave me an anxious look, and said, "Sonny's ex-girlfriend is pregnant."

"What!" I exclaimed, laying down my hot, buttered garlic bread. "You can't be serious."

Sonny's ex-girlfriend found out that she was pregnant after her breakup with him. I asked Tracy what she and Sonny had decided to do about the situation. She said that she really wanted to stay with him, but she feels like she is cursed when it comes to relationships, and now it's not just Sonny and her anymore, but the three of them, including the former girlfriend along with her baby, who represent a permanent link between the two even though they are no longer a couple. Tracy said she was feeling so hurt and confused that she didn't know how to handle this revelation.

"Why do these situations always happen to me?" she wondered. My response was that women in predicaments of that sort should allow troubled situations to unfold a blessing in their lives. I believe that you can see the true character of a man when his back is up against the wall, so problems and complications should be met squarely and dealt with openly. When the guy has nowhere to turn and must decide how to respond, what sort of decisions will he make? You may believe that these situations only happen because you don't deserve anyone who is "good" in your eyes, but these conflicts can happen to you because you "do" deserve someone who is good. Problems will either reveal the hidden value of a man when he comes under pressure, or they will show his weaknesses and thus give you the chance to leave the relationship before serious damage occurs.

I told Tracy she really needed to pay attention to Sonny. She should carefully note how he treats her. How is he treating his ex-girlfriend who is now pregnant with his child? What decisions is he making in response to his errors? She must pay very close attention to his actions, words, and attitude. She should consider a crisis as a blessing that will reveal his true ingredient label in their relationship so that she can make the best decisions in her own self-interests.

Melissa was another girlfriend of mine. She is what I would consider to be a free spirit, anything but conservative. Melissa would try anything once—and maybe twice! It was amazing when she decided to give a man a real chance, because relationships weren't a big deal to her. She could take them or leave them, and she mostly left.

But there was something about Alex that fascinated Melissa. She became very involved with him. At first, they had a really great relationship filled with mutual affection and respect, until Alex moved to another state to take a better job. All of a sudden, Melissa couldn't find Alex. He

Health Kick Sidebar:

I am a huge believer in interventions. I believe there are relationships in which we can become so entangled, we don't have the mental or physical strength to walk up out of them by ourselves. In these situations, I believe God intervenes and that how much we can bear becomes obvious. I always tell my girlfriends that I believe something will happen between you and your significant other that will be so nauseating that you will have no choice but to walk away. This will be a situation where your decision is made for you and there is nothing more that you can do at that time, but leave. Be prepared for those situations when you may feel overwhelmed and powerless, but understand that it could be happening for the good and not the bad.

wasn't as available to her as before. She had noticed that ever since he moved away, he had been rather distant with her, and said little during phone calls or text messages. She tried to trust him because she believed that even if they weren't together formally, their friendship would allow him to be honest with her regardless of any shifting circumstances. So one night she called him, and finally he answered his phone. Melissa took the opportunity to ask why he had been avoiding her. She said, "If you are seeing someone new, let me know—it's no big deal." He said she was being too emotional and assured her that nothing was going on. He was just busy. He then told her, for what seemed like the thousandth time, "I will call you back." Fifteen minutes later, as promised, her phone rang. She was shocked to see that it was him on the other line.

"Wow, you actually called me back?"

Alex didn't say anything at first. All of a sudden, Melissa heard Alex's voice in the background talking to Tommy, his best friend. For the next twenty minutes she listened diligently as he talked about how he wanted to be a better man with a girl he had been dating and how he was thinking of asking her to move in with him.

When Melissa told me this story, I was very sad to hear that Alex turned out to fall into Quadrant Four (the Enhanced Water) category, when she had really thought Alex belonged in Quadrant One (the Vegetable) category. Just as I'd advised Tracy, I told Melissa that she needed to change her perspective. The best way to look at the situation was to be thankful she had found out about Alex when she did. So many women are sitting at home wondering what is going on with the guy they are dating (or for that matter, the guy they are married to, like Erin). They would give anything to prove that he was cheating, if only to get peace of mind and the courage to make the final break in the relationship. Melissa was given all the proof she needed, and her decision was finally made.

Sometimes bad relationship discoveries lead to good outcomes. I always joke that the fastest way lose weight is to go through a breakup—I mean a good one, where you barely have an appetite. Although this is an extreme, please understand that there is a silver lining to everything that we go through. Information, whether positive or negative, is useful. Women must learn all they can about the men in their lives so they can obtain complete, accurate understanding to decide whether, and on what terms, to continue or end the relationship.

On this day of September 30, I solemnly vow to never go back to where I came from. I will never go back to the confusion, the hurt, and the pain that I felt while being with [him]. I vow to once again take control of my own emotions and to never give him a chance to hurt me again. I vow to never let another human being make me feel sorry for myself. I vow to never let another man come in and take my time, money, love and life away unless he is willing to share his with me.

~age twenty-three

Chapter Twelve:

When You Reach "Zero Tolerance"

During a girls' night to celebrate my birthday, Janelle decided to share with our group the story of her new relationship. She told us that she had reached a new level of relational maturity and personal accountability where she refused to tolerate ridiculous behavior from any man that she gives her time to. Janelle honestly expressed her outlook to the new guy she was dating and told him that she does not have time or energy to tolerate disrespect, neglect, abuse, or just plain foolishness. She genuinely apologized that he had to be the one to hear this speech, but explained that this would be the only time he would be subjected to a warning. Balancing between enthusiasm for maintaining the relationship and realism in accepting that her new guy might not share her views, Janelle basically told her guy that he might as well turn around and *walk*, because if irresponsible behavior was what he planned to bring to the table, she "ain't the one."

After everything that she had been through, Janelle finally reached Zero Tolerance (ZT). ZT is a threshold. It is a state of mind. It's a self-educational system that evolves from past experiences and responds rationally to present situations. ZT is happiness, maturity, and embracing one's higher values. It's a graduation from, "I may not yet know what I am looking for, but I know what I don't want," to, "Now I know what I'm looking for and I know what I need in my life." It is a state of understanding the ingredients of a man from the inside out. It's a pinnacle. It's a goal. It's a process of understanding.

ZT is where most women dream of being. You will know that you have reached Zero Tolerance when you not only say, "I don't have time for ridiculousness," but you also demonstrate it through appropriate boundaries and an effective response to problematic behavior.

ZT is not to be confused with bitterness. Let me explain the difference. A woman who is bitter has mentally given up on dating and relationships. Although she may physically go out with men and give her time to them, she is so emotionally insecure and withdrawn that the relationship has little chance of success. She automatically looks for, finds, and sometimes even magnifies a new guy's weaknesses and flaws rather than objectively assessing the whole person. ZT is the opposite, producing a more secure and connected woman. She is aware of her needs and wants in a relationship. She has an understanding of the ingredients that are necessary to have a healthy relationship, and she has developed the strength to hold out for the right man with a suitable combination of these necessary ingredients. She is not afraid to make her expectations known, nor to speak up when a man crosses a boundary. She is able to make a rational decision about when to offer a second chance and when to cut her losses and escape as fast as possible.

The million-dollar question is, "How do I get to Zero Tolerance?" I've seen a lot of women raised to understand that there are certain ways a man is to treat you. If he doesn't live up to those expectations, he is out of the picture. Steve Harvey describes his daughters in his book, *Act like a Lady, Think like a Man*. He tells readers how important it is to him that his daughters know what to look for in a healthy relationship and come to understand acceptable and unacceptable treatment between couples. His daughters are fortunate to have a caring, involved father to help guide their social development and relationship expectations. Sadly, many women lack either a father or mother to guide them through their formative years of interacting with the opposite sex. Consequently, many young women fail to develop the healthy boundaries and self-respect that are essential for enjoying positive relations with men. That is one of the reasons so many women today settle for loser boyfriends and abusive treatment. If these ladies would value themselves and expect others to do the same, they would have an excellent chance of finding a mate who would respect and care them for them in healthy and loving ways.

Many women have to learn relational self-defense the hard way. Following a string of abusive or broken relationships, they gradually become more mature; their difficult life experiences eventually drive them to Zero Tolerance. They've gone through so many bad relationships that they don't have the energy for another one. They would rather wait it out as a single woman before having the comfort of a man from the Cigarette quadrant.

I've known many women who get a whiff of a "good man" and refuse to take anything less in the next relationship. I recommend trying that. Date a Vegetable. Vegetables are known for treating women right the first time, and every time. Even if you are only dating a man casually, or if you would like to see what it feels like to not deal with drama for a little while, seek out a good-natured tomato or carrot and have some good, clean, old-fashioned fun. If there aren't any fireworks, at least you have less risk of going

---

Health Kick Sidebar:

I believe that you are being prepared for someone or something. Every time you are in a relationship that doesn't work out, it is preparing you for the one who will—even if it is by making you more sensitive for him, more tolerant of him, more patient with him, or whatever his needs may be. If it becomes clear that past failed relationships are not preparing you for the one special man who will fill your life with peace and joy, these situations are preparing you for something just as important, or more so.

home burned. By dating an open, honest, caring guy, some women can begin to see that positive relationships are possible, and they can use those wholesome dating experiences as a model of what to seek in a long-term relationship.

Some women, like me, are a combination of all of the above. During my rough dating years, older and wiser friends and relatives tried to give me helpful advice. Bad relationships ironically pushed me in the opposite direction, toward a wholesome dating experience. Setting a helpful example, my sister was in a great relationship, and I saw that it was possible to meet Mr. Right and avoid Mr. Wrong. And then to top it off, I got a whiff of a good man. Although he turned out to be within the Enhanced Water quadrant, I can never deny that he treated me better than his predecessors had, and our time together was unlike any other relationship before him. The moral of the story is that it doesn't matter how you make it there; what will matter is that you *arrive.*

Don't settle for fatty beef roast or rotten eggs, ladies. Read your man's ingredient label to find out exactly what he is made of before you let him into your life. And if you shop for the wrong guy or come home with a bad bargain, don't hesitate to throw him out and go back for the fresh, wholesome, delicious, and nutritious guy who will make you feel good.

Is what I want so hard to find? Maybe I should wait until I am, like, twenty-five or older. Maybe this will do me good. I have been looking for the perfect relationship ever since I knew what it was. Maybe my age could be the change that I need. But knowing me, I won't do it. I will just continue to get into bad relationships that eventually become a waste of time.

~ age twenty

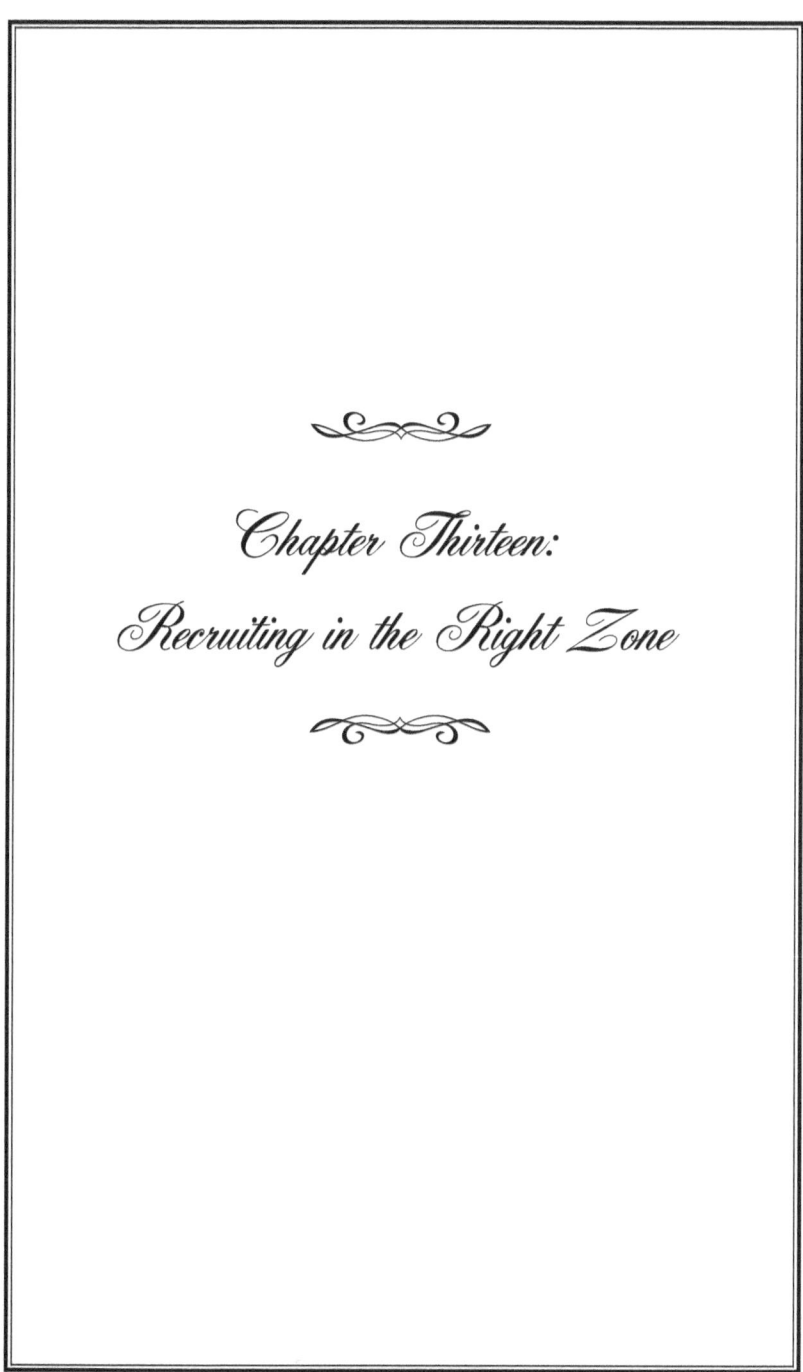

Chapter Thirteen:

Recruiting in the Right Zone

Once you realize you have Zero Tolerance for unhealthy relationships, it's time to start recruiting in the right zone. But let me explain some things first to prepare you for that possibility.

Although I enjoy writing as a hobby, I am a human resources professional by trade. Let me be more specific: I love human resources! Yes, I work in a department whose job is to enforce rules and advise other employees on what they can and can't do in order to keep the company from being sued. For the most part, I *love* my job. That's a little weird, right? I've been working within HR for a while, and currently I've landed a role recruiting for our company's nuclear division. To be honest, supporting our nuclear division sounds a lot harder than it really is.

Working with engineers, scientists, and nuclear operators has been such a learning experience that it seems almost more of a personal accomplishment than a job-related endeavor. The longer I am employed as a recruiter (regardless of the company), the more I am concerned that the managers I support have very little idea what they are doing from a hiring perspective. One of the main problems I have with my managers is that they don't understand the difference between basic qualifications and desired ones. For the benefit of this guide, I am going to explain the two and then bring my metaphor all together and make you say, "Oh, okay—*I get it now*!" Even better, you will begin to see how this affects my perception of male-female relationships.

First, a job description has three main parts: the description of the job, the basic qualifications, and the desired qualifications. The job description is exactly what it sounds like. It lists the duties or tasks that the employee will be responsible for handling day in and day out for that position. Anything listed under basic qualifications includes necessary knowledge, job skills, and relevant abilities needed to get the job done. Skills listed under desired qualifications are bonuses for the manager filling the position. These include the knowledge, skills, and abilities that may not be necessary to get the job done, but are qualities the manager feels will make a stronger employee, such as having an advanced degree or being able to type one hundred words per minute.

Here is the source of my frustration: At times, our company will have a few people apply for one position. At other times we will have hundreds—*maybe thousands*—of people apply for one position. In order to save time, many of my managers try to throw as many qualifications as necessary within their list of basic qualifications, hoping they will not have to sift through hundreds of applications in order to retrieve the best candidate. In theory, this is a great idea (aside from any legal implications), but in reality they end up receiving *no applicants*. Did you hear this? No one applies because no one feels qualified for this job. There are too many disparate requirements, and most aren't even necessary to be successful in the position. I wonder how many "super single" women are able to understand where I am going with this scenario.

Recruiting in the right zone means that you understand the matrix of men and quadrants, and now you are ready and open to begin looking for your ideal mate, regardless of the quadrant from which he hails. Before you can start recruiting in the right zone, you need to make sure you don't make the same mistakes my managers do. *Goodness*, I have girlfriends that do the exact same thing: try to squeeze too many "must haves" in a typical guy's ingredient label. We all know women who do this. These women think no one is good enough for them unless... (you fill in the blank). I have an inside joke with one of my girlfriends, Jasmine, about plumbers. Jasmine, now in her early forties, is single with high hopes that God will place a deserving man in her life one day very soon. Jasmine spends a lot of her spare time involved in church, so naturally I asked her if there are any single men there. She led me through the story of how there are a lot of them, but most are blue-collar men, like plumbers. She went on to say that she feels most of her church girlfriends who are in her same situation (mid-forties and single) have "settled" for the plumbers and other blue-collar men, but that she wasn't going to settle.

For the first time in a long time, I was taken aback by her personal opinion toward dating options. She and I have always been on the same page regarding dating and relationships. It sort of bothers me that Jasmine feels that these women (who are happy, by the way) have settled into marriages of convenience simply because the men are blue-collar professionals. In other words, Jasmine seems to think that many of her female church friends "lowered" themselves into marrying someone who is socially or professionally beneath them, based on income or career differences. But a blue-collar ingredient label may be hiding some fantastic inner qualities that any woman would love in her guy: faithfulness, diligence, respect, and great parenting skills. If so, Jasmine and women like her may be missing out on the opportunity to meet some truly deserving men because they will not "settle" for a guy in a blue-collar profession. By the way, a lot of Hot Peppers are blue collar men too.

If you are reading this, please listen closely: Do not take a man who may have landed in Quadrant Three, the Hot Pepper category, for granted. These men will probably turn your world upside down in a positive way. No person should be identified solely by profession. A profession is what you do; it's not who you are. One's character should never be judged exclusively by job choice. Your basic personal qualifications should respect his ambition to have a steady income instead of your desire for a guy to hold a certain professional status and making a certain amount of money.

Here is another example of a woman who is confusing basic and desired qualifications. Shanika was very confused about what she was looking for in a potential marriage partner. She dated Tony for a while. Tony was such a great man to Shanika. He would spend his last dollar to keep her smiling. He wanted to be in a relationship, he understood how to be faithful, he even did small things like open the door for her, take out her trash so she wouldn't have to go outside at night, and call her back when he said he would—and more. However, in the midst of the economy's woes, Tony happened to get laid off. Shanika started seeing a side of him that she didn't like. Tony wasn't in any rush to find another job. This would have been fine, had Tony been saving and preparing for a rainy day, but he hadn't. Being the driven person that Shanika was, she did all she could to help him find job openings, but he never applied to them. She constantly picked his brain to see if he was interested in finding work, and he would say yes, but then he would go back to playing video games. She came to me one day and expressed her feelings about Tony. She said that even if a job were to fall in Tony's lap and he were to be employed again, she knew that he might get laid off again, or even terminated. She was afraid that his behavior reflected a bigger problem that she didn't want to risk in the long run—*laziness*. They constantly argued about his laziness toward planning for his future and seeking employment. Shanika knew that this worried her more than anything, and she didn't like that feeling one bit. But she stayed in a relationship with him, despite her frustrations and concerns.

Shanika came to me one day and said that she knew I had to be wrong for believing that Tony's behavior was a "hiccup." She told me to look at the man that I was dating. She said that I joked all the time about how insensitive he was, and added, "He is not perfect, but you stay with him anyway." So, what is the big deal, right?

I explained that having a sensitive man for me is only a desired qualification. It would be a great bonus to our relationship if he wanted to cry with me once a month for no reason, or if he wanted to listen to *every* story that I tell him about how the girl on my job is trying to steal my position, but he doesn't. That is okay, especially because I have girlfriends to talk to. What he does do is protect me, provide for me, and desire a better-quality life and relationship as I do, and he ensures that I never go to sleep alone. That, to me, makes all the difference. Oh, he meets every basic qualification I have, and although it would be a bonus if he met every desired trait, he doesn't have to, because he is not perfect, and no person is—especially not me.

Shanika has it backwards. She believes that if a man has enough desired qualifications, these can overshadow the core qualities one needs in a relationship. She is wrong. Desired qualifications are a bonus, no matter which way you look at it. A man could have the body or the smile, he could wine and dine you every night, but if he doesn't have ambition, is he really what you are looking for? Now, I used that as an example; maybe ambition isn't a core trait for you. But the lesson is that you need to write out your basic and desired qualifications and become familiar with them so that you can screen anyone appropriately, consistently, and fairly—*like managers should do.*

I am not saying that Shanika is a foolish person for staying with this brother. What I am saying is that stability is a core for

Shanika. Stability is so much of a core that Shanika had it on her list of basic qualifications. She knew that her ideal mate would have to be someone who was driven. She knew that he needed to have the wherewithal to maintain himself even if he had to work three jobs until he was able to find his next career. Tony didn't have that one basic qualification, but he had almost all of her desired qualifications. Remember, I said that he took out her trash at night! He brought her lunch to work, sent her flowers, and watched her son's Little League games! Tony had it going on!

If you agree with Shanika, you are making the same mistake most of us make. Even though your man doesn't meet core requirements (substantive character qualities), you will continue to invest your time so that you can have all of your desired qualifications. In the end, you will find yourself breaking up with your Tony, "the apathetic," as Shanika finally did. She realized that she couldn't bring herself to let that all-important work-ethic quality go.

Now that you understand what a job description is and the importance of basic versus desired qualifications, it is time for you to build your own job description. What does it mean to be in a relationship with you? For example, I had to admit to myself that I need a lot of attention. Although this is something that I am working through, if someone wanted to be with me right now, this information would be an important part of my job description, because that is what it would really be like to be with me.

When you build your job description, write out a list of every quality you want and need in a partner. Spare nothing! These qualities are going to represent your basic and desired qualifications. I remember one of my girlfriends telling me that she had about a hundred items on her list. It was funny to hear some of the things she wanted from the future guy, such as a sharp haircut or going to the ballet with her. But if these traits are all-important, this is the time to find out! Keep writing—*get it all out of your system*!

What are those qualities you can't live without? What are your convictions about core qualities? After writing your list, put a star by those core qualities. I wanted someone who was seeking a commitment, who was ready to build a future with just one woman, who could share his space, display courtesy and use good manners, articulate a vision, and had similar forward-looking characteristics. My core list only dealt with character qualities, because those are the hardest things to change. You can't date someone based on their potential to change, because it may never happen. Is your basic qualification list complete?

Let's move on to the "desired" category. You want a man with a six-figure income, or you seek a gorgeous guy with six-pack abs. Put those on your list. As I mentioned earlier, everything under "desired qualifications" is only a bonus. If this man had nothing on your list of desired qualifications, he could still be just as good for you. Remember, desired qualifications are easier to change. You could help him find a better-paying job, advise him on how to dress better, and support him when he gets his teeth fixed, but you can't force him to have ambition if that isn't his core.

When your list is complete, keep it somewhere only you can see it. We don't broadcast or share lists. Read over it every now and again, but don't discuss it with anyone you are dating. Goodness, he would probably flee quickly if he knew that you had been looking specifically for him! After looking at your entire job description, decide which quadrant your ideal guy most likely would fall into. Does he appear to be more of the

Vegetable (Quadrant One), the Cigarette (Quadrant Two), the Hot Pepper (Quadrant Three), or the Enhanced Water (Quadrant Four)? How would he have come to be there? This means, what sorts of things would he have had to experience before he could demonstrate those core qualities you are seeking? An assessment like this can help you to determine which quadrant he falls into and whether he is a must-have or must-avoid.

Moving Forward

So now you have released all the baggage. You understand that you are not alone in your journey because most of us have gone through similar situations. At this point you have let the pain go, and you are open for a bright and better future. You know what you are seeking and how to recognize him. Good for you!

I, too, believe that when you have found the right guy, you will know it. Because you have gone through so many life experiences, by the time you do encounter the person with the ingredient label that is the best buy for you, you will recognize his worth and hold on tightly. There is no right or wrong to whomever you choose as long as he is treating you right and you are happy. You now know that this person does not have to be the most qualified person of all of the candidates who want your time, but he does need to be the best fit for you and your needs. You can even be with the Cigarette as long as you both are on the same page with the direction of your relationship. If you just want to have fun and he just wants to have fun, no strings attached, then why not?

When you have found him, there is a calming sense of satisfaction and serenity. This time you are realistic enough to know that you aren't perfect, and neither is he. You know that your relationship is not going to be a bed of roses every day, but you realize that both of you are involved and committed to each other's best interests. Music artist Heather Headly stated it best in her song when she said that love is full-time, overtime, and all the time. And everything is a lot easier when you are doing it together.

When the two of you have found each other, simply enjoy him and be blessed. Take the relationship one day at a time instead of grabbing his hand and running to the altar. Don't take your relationship too seriously. There will be time for serious moments, but be playful, laugh, and enjoy each other. Every decision is not a matter of life or death. Learn how to manage conflict. Try your best to hear him when the two of you are having problems. What is he saying to you verbally and non-verbally? What is he afraid to say, and why? The best advice I can give is that the two of you should set your own rules and create your own world. Learn from him and allow him to teach you as you grow together. Teach him, too. Without being overly judgmental, just love and be loved.

Health Kick Sidebar:

Hiring managers have a great system for finding the best person to hire, but if you plan to follow their steps, you must also be willing to do the difficult things they have to do, such as make a final hiring decision, ask those tough questions during interviews, explain to the rejected candidates why they weren't selected, and more. It comes with the territory, but the time spent is well worth it in the end.

I have plenty of wonderful things coming to me. I know I have a wonderful man who will be coming to me also. I can feel it! God loves me and I know that He will be taking care of me. At first I was really upset for this guy not giving me what I felt I deserved, but I will definitely be just fine. For now I need to be patient. I have goals and dreams and a strong mind and heart that will help me get exactly where I want to be. I have a beautiful destiny ahead of me that will take me exactly where I need to be. My life is good. I now know that I am ready to breathe. I am no longer scared of my future, but am more excited about it. It's amazing to me how easily I can see now if a man is no good for me. I now realize that I love me more than anything else. I can feel things. Soon I will be sitting in my own living room with my dog at my feet in my home with my wonderful job and my boyfriend calling on the other end of the ring while I am sitting back reading this journal entry. Things will be just fine. My life will be perfectly okay. I only have one more year left in school. Things will go well. I will smile a minimum of five times a day and laugh at least once a day … and maybe flirt some in the meantime.

– age twenty

Chapter Fourteen:
My Story

This is more than my story, it's who I am. No one ever taught me how to date or be in a relationship. As a matter of fact, you can see from my journal entries that I can't keep a man to save my life.

I grew up with a mother and a father in a stable home, with a relatively normal childhood, and with goals, dreams, hopes, and fears, and I still kept making the same mistakes as many other women do with the men in their lives. The more I think about dating and romance, the more I understand that my mistakes have less to do with my circumstances and more with my relationship education. What did I know about dating protocol and shopping for a mate? There really aren't as many effective playbooks out there for relationships as there are for sports (and diets, for that matter). That is why I have written my book: to fill the gap in women's understanding of love and appropriate attitudes and behavior.

It's not really my parents' fault, either, because no one ever taught them how to date or take care of a relationship. Commitment to another person is a perpetual cycle that just keeps manifesting in our culture as connective emotions between men and women. We've learned to talk about money, jobs, society, sex, drugs, and bullies when growing up. We have hopes as parents that this will be enough to prepare for the future, but it's not. When I turned sixteen and was allowed to date without supervision, no one ever said to me, "Here is how you date, here are the characteristics you should look for in a man, and here is what you should steer clear of."

I realize now that it was hard for many adults to envision the thought of my coming of age and being attracted to a guy. Sensitive issues like infatuation, physical attraction, sex, and commitment were not openly discussed when I was growing up, so it became trial and error for me as I matured. I would meet someone that I thought was superficially perfect with all the right masculine ingredients, fall for him overnight, and as I am packed and running to the marriage altar, I would look back and he would disappear. I would be left holding my baggage of embarrassment, anger, uncertainty, and sadness. For many years I did not understand why relationships had to end this way. Where were all the "happily-ever-afters" I had read about in fairy tales while growing up? Was my prince just an illusion? Or could I find him by carefully reading all the ingredient labels of the men who wanted to share my life, just as Cinderella's prince patiently tried to fit the abandoned glass slipper to all the maidens of the kingdom until he found the correct girl?

As a young woman, I mistakenly assumed that being a good man meant that he was a perfect man. I made the assumption that everything had to be right about him. But with time and errors, I learned that having a good man doesn't make him perfect! A guy can have many strong qualities that make him really good for you, and he may be exactly what you may need in your life, but that doesn't mean that he will not have flaws, just as you do. You may as well know right now that there's a good chance he will leave dirty clothes on the floor, forget to put the toilet seat down, and neglect his household chores until you nag him a bit. Of course, keep in mind that he will have to put up with your constant chatting or texting on the phone and incessant shopping expeditions. Not that these particular habits will apply, but they represent the kinds of behavior that can lead to tensions and arguments. It's best to expect such things to happen so when they do, you will be prepared to deal with them logically rather than emotionally.

I always thought my dad was perfect. It wasn't until I was older that I realized that although my dad was flawless in my eyes, he wasn't a perfect husband to my mother at all times. They were young when they married, and many of the things they learned about life and adulthood, they learned together. My mother and father's judgments about life and relationships went far beyond what I could digest until now. They made the decision to stay together through all of the good and bad times, because, ultimately, they were good for each other. They could recognize this and be satisfied to overlook the disappointments and frustrations.

My mom and I have such strong bond. If I ever go through a situation where I close down to the world, she is one of the few people who can really help me to come out of my slump. When I became an adult, around age twenty or twenty-one, my mom said two things to me that completely changed my perspective on dating and relationships. The first was, "Looks are going to hurt you."

She meant that looking from the outside in when searching for a boyfriend was going to be the cause of my struggle to find the man I prayed to share my life with. I spent a lot of time looking for the outwardly perfect guy to bring home to my family, until I realized it was the inside that I should have been searching for; that would have led to the most logical choice of partner. I would date men who looked like models, dressed like celebrities, held university degrees in subjects that I couldn't pronounce, were on their way to being the next executive in corporate America, and who looked or acted like Wall Street gurus. But what I didn't realize was that none of that would ensure that he would take care of me physically and emotionally. *And that is how this book came about!* Those "bling" qualities did nothing to assure me that he would want to be home with me, marry me, raise kids with me, and build a life together. That was my "Aha" moment.

The second thing my mother told me was, "Why would you want to find someone exactly like yourself? You are so busy trying to explore the world, write books, start businesses, and earn degrees, so what if he is doing the exact same things? Who will keep the two of you grounded? Who will be there to balance your life? Who will balance his?" I took both pieces of advice and allowed myself to begin searching for the right man from the inside out. I started searching for balance. I started searching for my mate.

I found my guy in Quadrant Three (the Hot Pepper). It was at a time when I least expected him. I almost pushed away my Hot Pepper because he came at a time when I was ready to give up. I said earlier that I can't keep a man to save my life, right? Even though we are in a solid relationship to this day, I am not keeping him here. *He is choosing to stay.* And as I said in the beginning, every day he has to make that decision in response to how he feels and what I do and say. So I try to make it easy for him without compromising my values and life goals. When people compliment us by saying that he and I are lucky to be together, I always remind them that we were lucky to have met, but being together was our decision—no luck was involved.

It's an amazing story to me, but I feel like he walked into my life and started walking in slow circles around me, picking up the pieces that my past relationships had left shattered. It wasn't his responsibility, and I don't even think he recognized what he was doing; I really believe that he wanted to see me happy. After my prior relationship had failed, my biggest concern was trying to figure out what to do with all the plans we had made, but all of those thoughts ceased when my new guy came. Guess what? We made new ones—better ones!

I recognized that he wasn't perfect just as he recognized my imperfections, but we are truly everything that we need in this season of our lives, and I pray that we will continue to be there for each other in seasons to come. No person can ever say that I don't know my man's worth, and I love that he knows how valuable I am. I love and respect him, and that's all I'm saying.

All of my relationship journeys have been necessary, as have yours. Do not be upset that you have gone through more broken relationships than your girlfriends have. Be upset when you haven't learned from them. Do not be jealous that you have to see your girlfriend and her boyfriend together and happy all the time. Be relieved that you are connected to them, which only means that you are close in line to find your individual happiness. Do not be bitter at your unhealthy past experiences; instead, be thankful that you can finally recognize them for what they are and can now recognize the warning signs that will help you avoid similar experiences in the future. You will find all that you deserve and more; just be patient. Best of luck to you! I'd love to hear your story when you "arrive!"

I'm truly blessed to have been able to experience all that I have at such a young age. It's more of a blessing to have an opportunity to spread this knowledge and pure inspiration to all of my sisters around the world. But unfortunately, there are some women and young girls that I won't be able to reach alone. It's not because I don't wish to reach them, but it's because the proper channel may not be available: She may not have the money to purchase this book, or the means to access the Internet or make it to the bookstore. Even if she can make it to the bookstore, or is able to purchase this book, she may not have the maturity to grasp the concept, or may not be in the place in her life where she feels comfortable reading this information.

But that is where you come in.

You can be the inspiration that she needs simply by making her aware that this book is available to her *and written for her.* "She" is any woman in need, whether it is your mother, sister, aunt, girlfriend, or even your fifteen-year-old niece who is ready to start dating. "She" may be hurting right now and you may be the only one who knows. You may be the only person who is able to reach her. Please do not look the other way because "she" is your responsibility too—she is your sister, even if you've never met. Don't keep this book to yourself; pass it along, or better yet, she deserves her own copy so that she can reference it in the future.

Pass this book along, even if it is to a stranger on the bus or to the lady sitting by you in the hair salon. Even if she doesn't look like she is walking up out of it, she may be—or better than that, "she" may be able to pass it along to a women's shelter, girls club, women's prison, crisis circle, etc.

Paying it forward is the easiest and most valuable gift you can give! Start today!

I invite you to contact to me at <u>me@jennifertardy.com</u> or visit my Web site at <u>www.JenniferTardy.com</u>. I would love to hear from you!

A Final Letter to my Sisters in Spirit

(Taken from my very first blog, Aug. 23, 2009)

With every passing minute, relationships are changing, lovers are becoming "just friends," tears are falling, anger is stirring, truths are being exposed and everyone involved is confused—again. In the end, women are becoming weary. Exhausted! "I can't do this again," rumbles another heartbroken woman.

In that passing minute, you moan to yourself, "Why does this keep happening to me?" Most of the time, it's probably because you keep taking him back. How can you expect anything different when you have always allowed the same (i.e., the same lies, same arguments, same neglect, etc.)? I wouldn't change if I were him either, especially if you've allowed it.

What's heartbreaking is that you believe that I am just talking to the "other" women, the ones who keep taking back their exes, but I am also focusing my attention on you. You, too, keep taking back the same man. Now, he may dress differently, speak with a different accent, hold you differently, and even promise you that he is better than every man before him. But when the truth is revealed, he is the same as all the others. He keeps promising you the same things, painting the same vision for your future together, and breaking your heart in the same way. Yes, believe it or not, you keep dating the same man over and over again.

Girlfriend, it's time for a change. Recognize who you are drawn to. What about him keeps hurting you? Is it his lifestyle, his desire for a "non-committed relationship," his popularity with other women? All of these things tell you about his character. If he displays the type of character that leaves you crying to yourself at night, tell yourself, "He won't work!" Remind yourself, "He won't work." Write it on your mirror if you have to. Find a new man, a better one.

And when your ex tells you that you will never find another man like him, just tell him, "I hope not!"

About the Author

A former native of Hurt, Virginia, J. M. Tardy grew up like any small-town girl. Creative and insightful, Jennifer has always been very curious about the big world around her. She graduated from Gretna High School and then went on to receive both her bachelor's and master's degrees from Virginia Tech, in Blacksburg, Virginia. She currently resides in Charlotte, North Carolina, where she works in the nuclear industry as a human resources professional. As an HR professional, J. M. Tardy's research has long been in understanding the behaviors of adults in the workplace. Her next goal is to further this research while attaining her Ph.D.

It wasn't until she realized that many of the single women that she knew seemed to be asking the same relationship questions, going through the same experiences, and justifying their actions with the same reasoning that she was able to make sense out of her own life experiences. It wasn't until recently that she even knew what her gift was: encouraging healthy relationships and healing broken hearts.

Her books stem from her personal research and the stories told by others. She wants each volume to grow as she grows and experiences new challenges in life. She knew that she had found the secret to healing a broken heart, but she didn't believe it was fair to just share this information with her girlfriends; she wants to share it with the world, and with this collection of books, she is sharing it with you.

Do You Have the Right Story?

I am very interested in hearing your story if you have ever experienced the scenario that I call, "walking-up-out-of-it." This notion is defined in Chapter Ten:

> *...with this option you will have to make a decision to walk away from your unhealthy relationship, like giving up smoking or fattening desserts. This will be a decision that will crush you in the beginning. I call this the "walking up out of it" phase."*
>
> *Walking up out of it is a decision that says you must get "through" it; you can't get "around" it. When you walk up out of it, this means that you don't know where you are going, or how you are going to get there, or if anything will be waiting for you when you arrive. All you do know is that the current problem situation is not where you are supposed to be in your life. This is not where you want to be, and you know that you deserve better. True, you will feel loneliness, sadness, pain, hurt, and perhaps even abandonment, but eventually these difficult emotions will be replaced with a sense*

of understanding, and eventually a sense of self-made happiness. Just know that you are going to go through withdrawal right now, but that will get better. People escape addictions all the time, and you can, too. Being a healthy consumer takes effort, but learning to select the best nutrients for your body and mind will restore a sense of ownership to your life and lead to healthy results in a short time, if you stick with it.

As for your former relationship, you still may have dozens of questions while you are walking up out of it. You may not understand what happened, why it happened the way it did, or what the future holds for the two of you. You may never know the truth of the matter, but because you are no longer blind or too emotional to be rational, you may begin to have a more balanced understanding of what took place. Understanding has always come to the patient and seeking ones, and it always will.

Can you relate to this? Have you ever been in an unhealthy relationship where you had it bad but didn't think you could leave? You would have done anything possible to keep him in your life, even though you *knew* that the relationship was toxic? If so, tell me your story. Also, tell me how you "walked up out of it." How did your relationship end? If your story was a long time ago, also send me an update on your current status.

What I am looking for:

  True stories
  Your personal story
  Length (2,000-5,000 words)
  Something different—not your average "he cheated and I left" story

What I am not looking for:

  Stories you've heard or someone else has experienced
  Multiple submissions (only send me your best story)
  Reprints (previously published stories)
  Fiction/poetry
  Inappropriate language (for example: references to a female as "slut," unless you are quoting someone)

To increase your chances of selection, please write in this format:

  Your background (preferably, at the time of the situation)
  Your story
  How you walked up out of it
  Your update (if applicable to you)
  Lessons learned

If you are selected, you will be contacted. Please send all submissions to me via e-mail at JenniferTardy@yahoo.com. I look forward to it!

www.ingramcontent.com/pod-product-compliance
Lightning Source LLC
Chambersburg PA
CBHW022253290526
45785CB00015B/767